# A WALKING TOUR
# Singapore

## G. Byrne Bracken

TIMES EDITIONS

All text and illustrations by **G. Byrne Bracken**
Editor: **Lynelle Seow**
Designer: **Ang Lee Ming**

**© 2004 Marshall Cavendish International (Asia) Private Limited**

Published by Times Editions – Marshall Cavendish
An imprint of Marshall Cavendish International (Asia) Private Limited
A member of Times Publishing Limited
Times Centre, 1 New Industrial Road, Singapore 536196
Tel: (65) 6213 9288    Fax: (65) 6285 4871
E-mail: te@tpl.com.sg
Online Bookstore: http://www.timesone.com.sg/te

Malaysian Office:
Federal Publications Sdn Berhad (General & Reference Publishing) (3024-D)
Times Subang
Lot 46, Persiaran Teknologi Subang
Subang Hi-Tech Industrial Park
Batu Tiga, 40000 Shah Alam
Selangor Darul Ehsan, Malaysia
Tel: (603) 5635 2191    Fax: (603) 5635 2706
E-mail: cchong@tpg.com.my

**National Library Board (Singapore) Cataloguing in Publication Data**
Byrne Bracken, G.
Singapore : a walking tour/G. Byrne Bracken ; [editor, Lynelle
Seow]. – 2nd ed. – Singapore : Times Editions, c2004.
p. cm.
First ed. published in 2002
Includes index.

ISBN : 981-232-630-8

1. Historic buildings—Singapore.  2. Historic sites —Singapore.
3. Singapore—Guidebooks.  I. Seow, Lynelle. II. Title.

DS608.8
959.57 — dc21                                SLS2004019345

Printed in Singapore by Times Graphics Pte Ltd

Dedicated to the memory of my aunt and uncle,
Marian and Charles Byrne.

# CONTENTS

# Acknowledgments

Thanks to all who have made the second edition of this book possible, but I would especially like to thank Lynelle Seow, who has been a wonderful editor and has done such sterling work on it, and Ang Lee MIng, for the art direction, excellent as always. Special thanks also goes to the Preservation of Monuments Board and the Malay Heritage Foundation for their comments.

# Introduction

Singapore is a tropical city, which means that walking would normally be hot and unpleasant but, thanks to the five-foot-ways that still line most of the streets in the historic districts and the generously-planted trees in the less urban areas, it's a relatively shaded and pleasant city to walk in. The city centre is also quite small and compact, with a number of beautiful urban and suburban colonial-era buildings in addition to modern works by some of the world's best architects.

Each chapter of this book presents one walk, and the chapters are organised as consecutive stops on one long route. They tend to cover one particular area per walk, except for Chinatown which is too large and had to be split in two. The buildings and sites listed are only suggestions for visiting; they don't have to be followed rigorously. Apart from the usual temples, mosques, churches and museums, there's also information on other places of interest, such as restaurants, bars, galleries and good views of the city.

Not all the roads have continuous paving, so be careful. Take rests, and don't overdo it in this weather. Drink plenty of liquids. There are plenty of shops, cafes and restaurants along most of the routes to stop and rest. If you wish to enter mosques and temples, you should dress appropriately (i.e. not in shorts and t-shirts).

# Note

## A Note on History

Sir Thomas Stamford Raffles, the founder of modern Singapore, drew up the original town plan, which divided Singapore along racial lines. According to the plan, the different ethnic groups lived in their own designated areas. His plan is still evident today in areas such as Chinatown and Kampong Gelam.

Chinatown rapidly became the largest of these areas due to its expanding immigrant population, most of whom came from China's southeastern coastal provinces. (After the 1871 opening of the Suez Canal, the Chinese population trebled between 1860 and 1900.) By this time, Chinatown was becoming increasingly overpopulated, rundown and squalid, and this pattern was to continue until the newly independent local government started massive housing programmes in the 1960s. During this time, huge tracts of Chinatown and the entire city centre were demolished to make way for new development. Many buildings of historical and cultural value were destroyed. The turning point came with the demolition of Raffles Institution (Singapore's top school) in the 1980s. The government then moved to a policy to rehabilitate and reuse buildings in historic districts. The conservation and restoration of these buildings saved much of Singapore's architectural charm and sparked off an urban renaissance.

## A Note on Spelling

Spellings of place and street names vary, as can be seen on maps, in guides and even on street signs. Those used in this guide are standardised with a preference for simple, accurate pronunciation.

## A Note on Architectural Style

Neoclassicism was universally popular in Singapore for government buildings, as it was in most of the British colonies right up until the outbreak of World War II, and yet the Gothic style reigned supreme in the United Kingdom during the same period. Why was that the case? It was often the younger sons of well-to-do families who went to the colonies to seek their fortunes. They were usually well-educated, which at that time meant classically-educated, and they favoured the neoclassical style, maybe due to a lack of architectural imagination or for nostalgic reasons.

Gothic was the preferred architectural style of the self-made industrialists from the North of England, who began to have more of a say in the running of the United Kingdom as the 19th century wore on, influencing the style of government buildings, including the Houses of Parliament at Westminster. The neoclassical style is a balanced, well-ordered and tidy-looking one, and was a fitting image for a colonial government.

# South East Asia

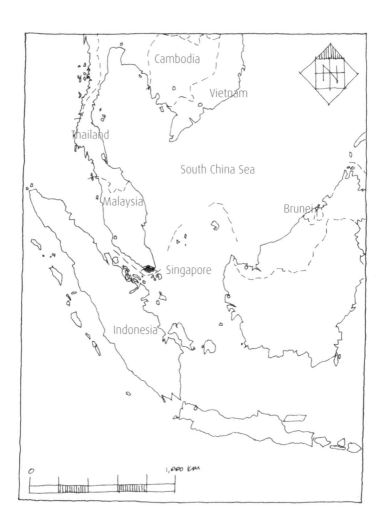

# Singapore

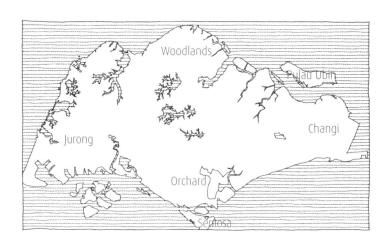

## A Note on Icons

To inform readers about the interesting features of the places mentioned in the book, we have added icons, drawn by the author, to represent the following:

 Must See

 National Monument

 Good View

 See At Night

 Drinking

 Eating

 Shopping

# Checklist

Sunglasses.
Sun screen.
A small umbrella for the frequent Singapore showers, it can also come in useful as a parasol.
A small hand towel.
A bottle of something to drink is essential.
Tiger Balm when applied promptly to mosquito bites is extremely effective in preventing them from itching and becoming inflamed.

"The city of Singapore was not built up gradually, the way most cities are, by a natural deposit of commerce on the banks of some river or at a traditional confluence of trade routes. It was simply invented one morning early in the nineteenth century by a man looking at a map."

—J.G. Farrell, *The Singapore Grip*

# Chinatown West

**Nearest MRT: Outram Park**
**Approximate walking time: 45 minutes**

## Bukit Pasoh & Kreta Ayer

Chinatown consists of four sub-districts. This first walk covers Bukit Pasoh and Kreta Ayer, which were developed in the 1830s and the early 1900s, respectively. The other two areas of Chinatown — Telok Ayer and Tanjong Pagar — were developed in the 1820s and the 1920s.

# THE WALK

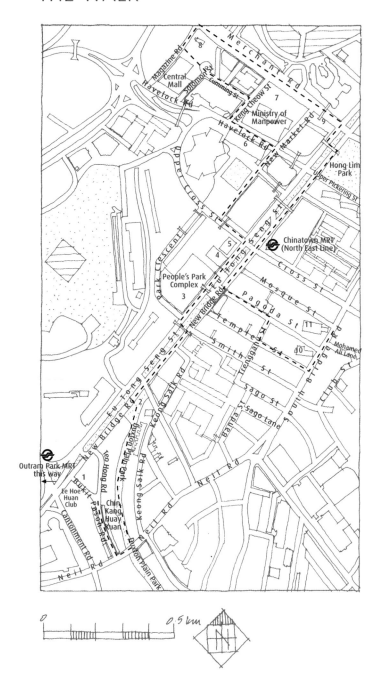

# KEY

1. Bukit Pasoh Road

2. Duxton Plain Park

3. People's Park Complex

4. The Majestic

5. Yue Hwa Department Store

6. Family and Juvenile Courts

7. Omar Kampong Melaka Mosque

8. Tan Si Chong Su Temple

9. Thong Chai Medical Institution (Former)

10. Sri Mariamman Temple

11. Jamae Mosque

Chinatown West

Bukit Pasoh Rd

## Bukit Pasoh Road. . . .

Number 21 Bukit Pasoh Rd is one of a row of three-storeyed Late Style shophouses. № 30 (c. 1928) is at the centre of a fine art deco terrace. Walking with your back to the Outram Park MRT, the Ee Hoe Hean Club, founded in 1895 and one of the oldest millionaires' clubs in Singapore, can be spotted on your right. Farther down on your left is the Chin Kang Huay Kuan, established in 1918 by Chinese immigrants from the southern Fujian county of Jin Jiang, China. The headquarters of the Overseas Chinese General Mobilisation Council, it was formed in 1941 to help defend Singapore against the Japanese. The nearby Keong Saik Rd, roughly parallel to Bukit Pasoh Rd on the left, is home to about 30 Chinese cultural and clan associations (*kongsi*), which were often affiliated with *tongs* (secret societies). As a result, this street was nicknamed the "Street of Clans".

## Duxton Plain Park. . . .

Turning the left corner at Neil Rd, you will encounter the unusually shaped Duxton Plain Park. This odd shape was a result of the realignment of the Malayan Railway in the 1930s. The railway line — which used to cut across Chinatown (and continued north toward Orchard Rd) — was removed, leaving this unusual, elongated park.

21 Bukit Pasoh Rd

## Note: Kreta Ayer

When you emerge out of the park, turn right and walk along either Eu Tong Sen St or New Bridge Rd. You will be approaching Kreta Ayer, traditionally the hub of the Chinese community, located between New Bridge and South Bridge Roads and consisting of Smith, Temple, Pagoda, Trengganu and Sago Sts.

Literally "water cart" in Malay, Kreta Ayer takes its name from the buffalo carts that used to carry water to this area. This land was once owned by the wealthy Portuguese d'Almeida family. South Bridge Rd was damaged by fire in 1830. It used to experience knee-high floods during high tides. A steam tram used to ply this street between 1885 and 1894. An electric tram also operated here between 1905 and 1927, during which time the street was extensively rebuilt.

Yue Hwa Department Store

## People's Park Complex. . . .

After passing Smith St on the right and Park Crescent on the left, you will arrive at People's Park Complex. Built in 1970, it consists of 31 storeys of offices and apartments above a shopping centre. It was the first building of its type in Southeast Asia, providing a model that has been much copied throughout the region. The building is somewhat dated, but is one of the best places in Singapore to get a feel of modern-day Chinatown.

## The Majestic. . . .

Farther down on the your left, you will pass a colourful Chinese art deco shopping centre. Originally called Tien Yien Moh Toi and used for Cantonese opera, it was built in 1927 for Eu Tong Sen (a prominent tin miner and rubber planter) and designed by Swan & Maclaren. When it was a cinema, it was named the Queen's Theatre before it was called the Majestic Theatre.

## Yue Hwa Department Store. . . .

The next building you will pass on your left was the tallest building in the area in the 1930s. The well-proportioned Yue Hwa Department Store is reminiscent of some of the work of the early modernist architects. The decorative metal work on the 5th and 6th storeys has been painted an attractive green. Built by Swan & Maclaren in 1936, it was formerly the Great

Southern Hotel and the first Chinese hotel to have a lift. It's now a good place to buy imported Chinese goods.

## Family & Juvenile Courts. . . .

Turn left onto Upper Cross St and then right into the carpark, and you will see the Family & Juvenile Courts building. Designed by H. Stallwood of the Public Works Department in about 1923, this neoclassical building started life as the Chinese Protectorate Building. An imposing, formal and symmetrical building, it was home to the Ministry of Labour until 1990 and is now the Family and Juvenile Courts.

Note: The Chinese Protectorate
William A. Pickering (1840–1907), the first Chinese Protector, came to Singapore in 1872 after having spent eight years in China. He was the first European official who could speak and read Chinese (he was fluent in written and spoken Mandarin as well as various Chinese dialects). He established the Chinese Protectorate in 1877 to protect Chinese coolies (unskilled labourers), who were often ill-treated in Singapore. He held the post for 12 years, retiring early after an attempt on his life seriously injured him and left his confidence shaken. (His efforts to curb the activities of the Chinese secret societies had made him many enemies.) Pickering was regarded by the Chinese as a benefactor and was known as a *daiyan* (Cantonese for "great man"). For a long time after his death the Chinese Protectorate office was known simply as "Pi-ki-ling".

## Omar Kampong Melaka Mosque. . . .
Turn left on Havelock Rd, the road beyond the Family & Juvenile Courts Headquarters. Walk down this road and turn right onto Keng Cheow St. Just after the Ministry of Manpower building, halfway down this street, you will come to the Omar Kampong Melaka Mosque on the right. This was the site of the first mosque on the island. It began as a temporary building in 1820 and was rebuilt in brick after roads were built at the end of the 19th century. This current mosque, constructed in 1920, is the third on the site. It's a simple building in an attractive urban environment. It underwent considerable reconstruction in the 1980s, including the addition of a dome and minaret.

Godown on Magazine Rd

# Tan Si Chong Su Temple. . . .

The road facing the Omar Kampong Melaka Mosque is Cumming St. Follow this until you get to a small square in front of Central Mall. Cross this square and follow the covered pedestrian passageway out onto Magazine Rd. Turn right past the godown (warehouse), and you will arrive at Tan Si Chong Su Temple. This single-storeyed Hokkien temple, built in 1876 as the ancestral temple and assembly hall for the Tan clan, is also known as Po Chiak Keng. The main donors for its building were Tan Kim Cheng and Tan Beng Swee. Located in an area that once housed many godowns, it is close to the Singapore River, supposedly lending it favourable feng shui. Rich in gilt-covered decorative carvings, mouldings and murals imported from China, the building's layout, with its sequence of two courtyards and worship halls, reflects the Chinese etiquette of *li* (the manner of humbling oneself in deference to other people).

## Note: Feng Shui

Pronounced "fung shuay" in Singapore, and also called geomancy, it translates as "wind water". A vital consideration even in the most modern constructions, it is the art of arranging the physical environment to harmonise with the nature of the individual or group. Water is equated with wealth. Doors, walls and furniture must be aligned according to its principles to prevent good spirits, wealth and harmony from flowing out. Straight lines and sharp corners are generally avoided. Bad feng shui can be corrected by using wind chimes, trigrams, mirrors or plants.

# Thong Chai Medical Institution (Former). . . .

Continue to the end of Magazine Rd, turn right onto Merchant Rd, and follow it all the way to Eu Tong Sen St. At the junction, you will find the former Thong Chai Medical Institution on your right. Built in 1892, largely through the endowment of Gan Eng Seng, a Malacca-born philanthropist, this was the best known of the Chinese charity medical centres. *Thong chai* means benefit to all. Traditional Chinese doctors (*sinsehs*) gave out free treatment and medicines to all races in Singapore here. (During the 1911 malaria outbreak, quinine was given to the poor.)

Originally established in 1867, the Thong Chai Medical Institution was first housed at 31 Upper Macao St (now Upper Pickering St). It was later moved to this custom-built two-storeyed hospital building. Constructed in a Chinese palace style, it consists of two inner courtyards containing decorative carvings. It's one of the few non-religious, Chinese-style buildings left in Singapore. For a good view of this building, climb the pedestrian bridge over Eu Tong Sen St and New Bridge Rd.

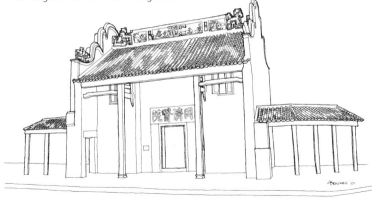

Thong Chai Medical Institution (Former)

# Sri Mariamman Temple. . . .

Descending near Hong Lim Park, follow New Bridge Rd to Pagoda St, the fifth street on the left. Halfway down Pagoda St, turn right onto Trengganu St and then left onto Temple St. Walk along Temple St until you reach South Bridge Rd. Turning left onto South Bridge Rd, you will see the Sri Mariamman Temple, the oldest Hindu temple still in use in Singapore. The temple, built in 1827 by Naraina Pillai, was originally made of timber and thatch . (Pillai had travelled down from Penang with Raffles, and he subsequently founded Singapore's first brickworks.) The present Dravidian-style brick temple was built by Indian convict labour between 1827 and 1847. The colourful *gopuram* was made by craftsmen from India and was modelled after South Indian Tamil temples. The cow is a prominent decorative feature. The temple is dedicated to the Indian goddess Mariamman, who is invoked during epidemic illnesses.

Jamae Mosque

# Jamae Mosque. . . .

Farther down South Bridge Rd, between Pagoda and Mosque Sts, is the
Jamae Mosque. This was built between 1827 and 1835 by *chulia* (or *jamae*)
Indians (Muslim merchants from South India). Also known as the Indian
Mosque, this building has a simple layout and is an eclectic mix of Chinese,
Anglo-Indian and Malay architecture. Its obelisk-like towers are capped by
small domes and consist of pairs of small niches with horizontal mouldings
between them. The prayer hall is located within an airy courtyard whose
arched openings are moulded and filled with fine Malay timber fretwork.

*Link to the Chinatown East walk: Cross South Bridge Rd. Opposite Jamae*
*Mosque is Mohamed Ali Lane. Follow this lane until it opens out onto Club St*
*beside an outdoor carpark.*

# Chinatown East

**Nearest MRT: Raffles Place**
**Approximate walking time: 45 minutes**

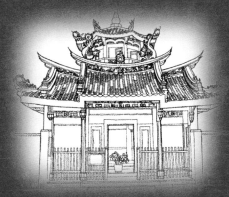

## Tanjong Pagar & Telok Ayer

Tanjong Pagar's name derives from the wooden fishing stakes used by the *orang laut* (native fishermen) who lived here before it was converted into plantations by the Europeans and the Chinese. The opening of the New Harbour (now Keppel Harbour) led to the area's economic development and made it a gateway for Chinese immigrants. Living conditions were often overcrowded, coolies often shared bed space and lived in subdivided cubicles. Tanjong Pagar was an area humming with activity; with craftsmen, coolies, opium smokers, rickshaw pullers, port workers and ladies of the night going about their business.

# THE WALK

See detailed map on page 32

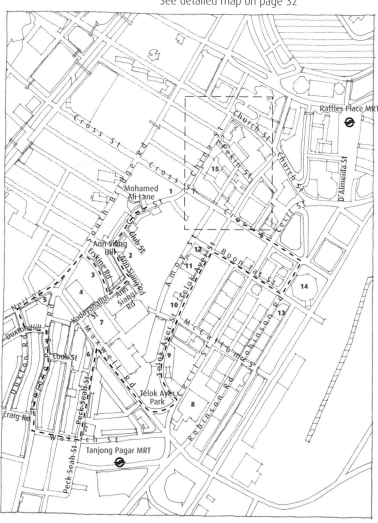

0.5km

# KEY

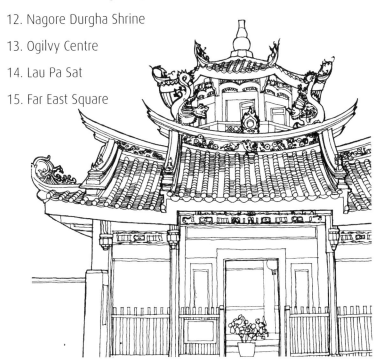

Club St

## Club Street. . . .

If you are walking from Raffles Place MRT, leave via D'Almeida St. Turn right onto Cecil St and follow it as it curves to the left, crossing Church St. Take the next right onto Cross St, following it until you come to Club St, the third street on your left. Club St was named after the Chinese Weekly Entertainment Club, founded in 1892 by a Peranakan millionaire and located on neighbouring Ann Siang Rd.

This is a busy area, home to up-market offices and restaurants. There's a large, well-proportioned and colourful art deco building on Mohamed Ali Lane. Facing this is a small imaginative apartment building, designed by Frank Brewer in 1932. This now forms the entrance to a condominium complex (sadly out of scale with the rest of the area.) Look out for the laneways in this area with their barbers under tarpaulin and their mirrors hanging on the old crumbling walls.

## Ann Siang Road. . . .

Turn left off Club St onto Ann Siang Rd and follow it uphill. Originally called Scott's Hill, Ann Siang Rd was the site of the first Anglo-Chinese School. Opened by Reverend Oldham in 1886, it was the first in a chain of Methodist schools in Singapore. This intimate street curves its way up a gentle hill, and its staggered junction with Club St creates a delightful urban space more reminiscent of the Mediterranean than of Asia.

## Erskine Road. . . .

Turn right off Ann Siang Rd onto Erskine Rd. Erskine Rd was probably named after J.J. Erskine, a Member of the Legislative Council in Penang in 1824. Despite the destruction wrought at its South Bridge Rd end, it's still one of the more charming streets in the city, consisting of a terrace of two-storeyed shophouses — some of which are currently being converted into a hotel — that step their way confidently up a gently curving slope At the junction of Erskine Rd and Ann Siang Rd is a fine art deco corner building. The street contains a good mix of both the Early style (Nºs 7–13) and First Transitional style (Nºs 15 onward) shophouses.

Erskine Rd

## Maxwell Road Food Centre. . . .

At the lower end of Erskine Rd, turn left onto South Bridge Rd and walk towards Maxwell Rd, where you will see the Maxwell Rd Food Centre. Formerly known as the Maxwell Market, this single-storeyed neoclassical building with its simple industrial roof structure is home to a hawker food court. It was completely renovated in 2001.

## Jinricksha Building. . . .

Nestled on the corner of Neil Rd and Tanjong Pagar Rd is the Jinricksha Building. Built in 1903 by the Municipal Council, this was the city's administrative centre for rickshaws. This building has a gently tapering square tower and octagonal cupola. The Ionic pilasters and curved corner pediment are also attractive. The exposed brickwork façade is original and would have been considered a most unusual feature at the time.

Slightly farther along Neil Rd is the Tea Chapter, an intimate tea shop, also home to a small museum dedicated to tea. (Incidentally, Neil Rd in Chinese used to be called Gu Chia Chwi Kia Lo or "The Steep Street of Kreta Ayer".)

> **Did You Know?**
> Originally invented in Japan, the rickshaw (also spelt *jinricksha*) was introduced to Singapore from Shanghai around 1880. By 1919, there were 20,000 rickshaw pullers in the city, and they continued their trade until just after World War II, when rickshaws were replaced by trishaws.

**Tea Chapter (Tea Museum and Shop)**
9a–11a Neil Rd. Tel: 6226 1175. Open from 11am to 11pm daily

Chinatown East

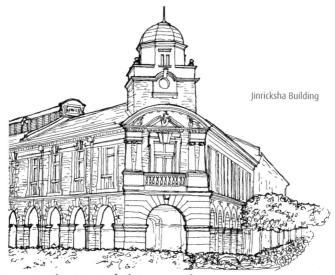

Jinricksha Building

# New Asia Hotel (Former). . . .

Continue up Neil Rd, turn left onto Duxton Rd, left again at Duxton Hill, and right down Tanjong Pagar Rd. Passing Cook St on your left and Craig Rd on your right, turn left onto Wallich St. Take the second left turn down Peck Seah St. At the end of this street is an office building that used to be the New Asia Hotel, restored in 2000. Designed by Chung and Wong in 1930, this attractive building would not look out of place even in Shanghai.

# URA Centre. . . .

Facing the New Asia Hotel across Maxwell Rd is the URA (Urban Redevelopment Authority) Centre. This Kenzo Tange building, completed in 1998, consists of two blocks. The main entrance is located in the long elegantly curved wing facing Maxwell Rd. The rear block is tall but less interesting architecturally. They are both linked by a narrow but airy atrium. The first storey has a public office containing planning information, where books and maps are for sale. The 2nd and 3rd storeys contain a public gallery with planning information about the future (and past) of Singapore. It also contains an impressive 11-by-11-metre (36-by-36-foot) model of the city centre, which even shows plans for the future expansion of the city.

### Public Gallery, URA Centre

2nd floor, URA Centre. 45 Maxwell Rd. Tel: 6321 8321
http://www.ura.gov.sg
Open from 9am to 4:30 pm, Mon–Fri and 9am to 12:30 pm, Sat.
Admission: Free

# Capital Tower. . . .

With the URA Centre on your left, continue down Maxwell Rd, turning the bend with Telok Ayer Park on your left. Capital Tower will loom directly ahead. This 52-storeyed building, completed in 2000 by Singaporean firm RSP Architects, has an unusual tapering profile. The sheer scale and

monumentality of its form lends it considerable urban presence and allows it to act almost like a gatepost at the southern entrance of the Central Business District. Its penthouse is home to the posh China Club.

## Telok Ayer Chinese Methodist Church. . . .

Take a sharp left down Telok Ayer St. You will see the Telok Ayer Chinese Methodist Church on the right. Built in 1924, its origins can be traced to a rented shophouse on Japan St (now Boon Tat St). An unusual and attractive building, it's dominated by the squat, centrally placed tower which has a rather exaggerated Chinese roof. This vaulted church is lit through large, arched, almost Byzantine-style windows. There's a continuous tiled loggia on the top storey.

## Al-Abrar Mosque. . . .

Walk down Telok Ayer St and past the junction of Amoy St and McCallum St, and you will find the Al-Abrar Mosque. Also known as *Kuchu Palli* (meaning the "Hut Mosque" in Tamil), this brick building probably began life as a thatched hut. Built between 1850 and 1855, it is simpler in style than the earlier mosques of Singapore. It mixes Indian and Islamic architectural elements. The narrow, and rather plain, frontage is dominated by two tapering towers (with two smaller ones in between) topped by small, onion-shaped domes (*chatri*).

Thian Hock Keng Temple

## Thian Hock Keng Temple. . . .

Farther down Telok Ayer St, on the left, is the Thian Hock Keng Temple. Meticulously restored in 2000, this is the oldest Chinese temple in Singapore and the most important temple for Hokkien Buddhists. Chinese immigrants used to offer thanks to Ma-Zu-Po (or Ma-Cho-Po), Goddess of Seafarers, for a safe voyage at a joss house here as early as 1821. Her statue, imported from mainland China in 1840, can still be seen in the main hall. Largely financed by Malaccan-born pioneer and philanthropist Tan Tock Seng, it was built between 1839 and 1842 with materials from China. Traditionally laid out, it was on the seafront until the land reclamation of the 1880s. The craftsmanship is excellent, with elaborately decorated hardwood roof forms and unique structural elements (such as columns carved from solid blocks of granite in the form of entwined dragons). The cast iron railings came from Glasgow, Scotland and the decorative tiles from Delft, Holland.

> **Did You Know?**
> Another name for the Thian Hock Keng temple was the Temple of Heavenly Happiness. This name was rather ironic as a slave trade was reputedly carried out here in the 1850s. In 2001, the temple won Honourable Mention in the UNESCO Asia-Pacific Heritage Awards for Cultural Heritage Conservation.

## Nagore Durgha Shrine. . . .

At the junction of Telok Ayer St and Boon Tat St, you will find the Nagore Durgha Shrine. This shrine was built by *chulias*, between 1828 and 1830, in memory of Shahul Hamid, a devout Muslim. The building's form is reminiscent of that of the nearby Jamae Mosque. It freely mixes Western classical motifs (like the arcade) with Muslim Indian ones (such as the decoratively perforated parapet).

Ogilvy Centre

## Ogilvy Centre. . . .

Turn right and walk down Boon Tat St. Just after the Robinson Rd junction is the Ogilvy Centre on your right and Lau Pa Sat on your left. First known as the Cable and Wireless Building, and then the TAS Building, it was designed in 1927 by F.G. Lundon of Swan & Maclaren. It is a robust neoclassical structure with large Ionic columns and recessed balconies.

## Lau Pa Sat. . . .

Formerly the Telok Ayer Market, this distinctive octagonal building was made of cast iron from the Glasgow firm of P. & W. MacLellan and erected by Riley Hargreaves and Company (now United Engineers Limited). Built in 1894 on reclaimed land, it was designed by municipal engineer James MacRitchie to replace an earlier market, also octagonal, by Singapore's first architect — G.D. Coleman. Originally a fish market, Lau Pa Sat is located on what used to be the waterfront. (*Telok* and *ayer* are Malay words for *bay* and *water*.) Converted into a food centre in 1973, it was carefully dismantled during the construction of the MRT line in the 1980s and then reassembled.

## Far East Square. . . .

With Lau Pa Sat on your right, walk along Robinson Rd until you get to Cross St. Turn left down Cross St, passing three streets on your left before coming to Far East Square on your right. (Detailed map of Far East Square on page 32.) This is a partially roofed shopping and restaurant complex which stretches over the city block between Telok Ayer, Pekin, China and Cross Sts. The original street layouts and building façades have been retained and converted into a shopping centre, with some additional modern features, such as a partially glazed retractable roof.

## Chui Eng Free School. . . .

Now home to restaurants and popular nightspots, including the Boom Boom Room, this is where one of the first free schools in Singapore used to be located. After a century, it was incorporated into the Hokkien Huay Kuan list of sponsored schools in 1954.

Chui Eng Free School

Chinatown East

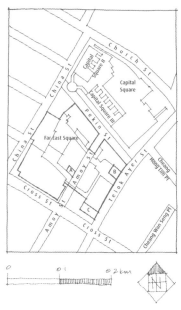

**Key: Far East Square**

A. Chui Eng Free School
B. Fuk Tak Ch'i Museum
C. Ying Fo Kui Kun

## Chui Eng Free School
131 Amoy St. Tel: 6532 7868. Open from 10am to 10 pm daily.
Admission: Free

# Fuk Tak Ch'i Museum. . . .
Built in 1824 and reputedly the first Chinese temple in Singapore, this is now a museum. Its courtyard is well-proportioned and rich in *hu lu* roof decoration. Its main deity was Tua Peh Kong (or Da Bo Gong), the God of Wealth. Laid out on axial lines, it was originally oriented toward the sea. Standing on the site of an earlier temple dating from 1820, its religion was syncretic. Called Fu An Miao in Mandarin, this temple was originally painted red and white.

## Fuk Tak Ch'i Temple Museum
76 Telok Ayer St. Tel: 6532 7868. Open from 10 am to 10 pm daily.
Admission: Free

# Ying Fo Fui Kun. . . .
Built in the early 1880s, this two-storeyed building, with a small open-air courtyard, houses a Hakka association for the Khek community. Founded by Liew Loon Teck in 1882, there is a shrine to Kuan Ti, the God of War, on the upper floor.

## Ying Fo Fui Kun
98 Telok Ayer St. Open from 9am to 5pm, Mon-Sat. Admission: Free

*Link to the Singapore River walk: Head north in the direction of Church St. Turn right and walk along Church St until it merges with Cecil St. You will soon see Raffles Place on your left.*

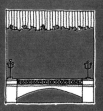

# Singapore River

**Nearest MRT: Raffles Place**
**Approximate walking time: 45 minutes**

## Singapore River

The Singapore River was the commercial life-blood of the colony. Today, the area is Singapore's commercial and entertainment hub. Raffles landed on the north side of the river in 1819. He recognised the river's importance and ordered that the north bank be drained as a site for government buildings. The swampy south bank was also drained to make way for a Chinese settlement. The south bank was said to have had good feng shui, and the Chinese settled in that area. The Malays lived in *kampongs* (villages) farther upstream, while the Indians moved to areas such as Rochor, Kallang and Geylang.

# THE WALK

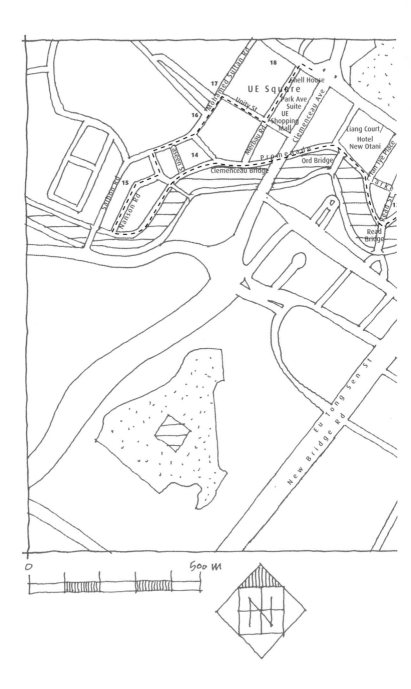

Singapore River

# Key

OUB Centre

# Raffles Place. . . .

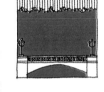

When you emerge from the Raffles Place MRT, you will find yourself in Raffles Place. Originally known as Commercial Square, it was renamed Raffles Place in the 1850s. At that time, merchants could look across the newly built sea wall at Collyer Quay to keep an eye on their ships. This square used to contain many splendid 2- to 4-storeyed buildings, including the John Little Department Store. (John Little's decorative gable has been imitated for the entrances to the Raffles Place MRT station.) Many of these buildings bore the handiwork of G.D. Coleman.

Shady flame-of-the-forests trees, ponies, rickshaw-pullers and Bengali coffee vendors used to fill in the rest of this urban canvas at the beginning of the 19th century. Then, offices along Collyer Quay had elongated verandahs along the seafront. By the time the square was pedestrianised in 1972, most of the old buildings had gone. Some of their replacements are architecturally quite good, notably Kenzo Tange's OUB Centre, but none really improves the urban character of the square.

## OUB Centre. . . .

On the western side of Raffles Place is the 63-storeyed OUB Centre. Built in 1986 by Kenzo Tange, it was the tallest building in Asia when it was completed. The building is a basic square that has been made to look like two triangles, one rising 13 storeys above the other, giving quite an elegant appearance to an otherwise bulky building. At 280 metres (919 feet), it's one of the three tallest skyscrapers on the island. (The other two are the 66-storeyed Republic Plaza, built in 1995 by Kisho Kurokawa, and the 66-storeyed United Overseas Bank Plaza 1.) Due to air traffic regulations, 280 metres is the highest one can build in Singapore.

## Clifford Pier. . . .

Across Raffles Place from the OUB Centre, is a covered pedestrian walkway called Change Alley. This will take you onto Collyer Quay, opposite Clifford Pier. There is a pedestrian bridge here which you can use to get to Clifford Pier. Chief Architect of the Public Works Department, F.D. Ward, designed this simple and well-detailed landing point to replace the old Johnston Pier. Named after Governor Sir Hugh Clifford of the Straits Settlements, it was opened in the early 1930s.

## One Fullerton. . . .

Leaving Clifford Pier, turn right and you will see One Fullerton ahead of you. Designed by Architects 61, this interesting and attractive low-rise structure overlooks Marina Bay and is home to a number of restaurants, cafes and clubs, all nestling elegantly under the waves of its gently curving roofs. It is connected to the Fullerton Hotel via an underground link.

Singapore River

# The Merlion. . . .

Continue along the waterfront, and you will see the Merlion statue along Marina Bay ahead of you. Consisting of the body of a lion with a mermaid's tail, it was completed in 1972 and originally stood in what used to be Merlion Park on nearby Fullerton Road until the recently constructed Esplanade Drive stranded it inland. It is Singapore's national logo and is symbolic of the ancient city of Temasek, as Singapore was then known. It moved to its present position in 2002.

# The Boathouse. . . .

Continue along the waterfront and under the Esplanade Drive and you will see The Boathouse on your left. Formerly known as the Waterboat House, it was originally the Port of Singapore Authority and was built by Swan & Maclaren in 1919. Recent land reclamation has left it well inland. An elegantly curved art deco stone structure with distinctly nautical lines, it has recently been restored and extended to include a giftshop and restaurant.

# Fullerton Hotel. . . .

Cross Fullerton Road and follow the riverside walkway and you will see the Fullerton Hotel on your left.

**Did You Know?**
During the Japanese Occupation, the Japanese used to display the severed heads of looters on poles in front of the Fullerton building.

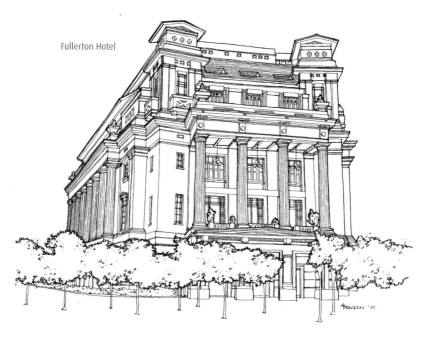

Fullerton Hotel

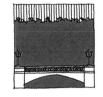

Fort Fullerton (c.1829) once stood on what is now the northern end of the Fullerton Hotel. This fort was demolished in 1873, and the Victorian-styled General Post Office was built in its place. (The road, this building and the square are all named after Robert Fullerton, who was a governor of Singapore in the 1820s). The tax office for a brief period, it was rebuilt in a neoclassical fashion in 1928 as the Fullerton building by the firm of Keys & Dowdeswell. Its top floor used to house the exclusive Singapore Club. It is said that the British hid a Union Jack here throughout the Japanese Occupation. In 2000, it became the luxurious Fullerton Hotel, which has an underground link to One Fullerton.

## Bank of China. . . .

Continue along the waterfront, and you will see the Bank of China on your left. Built by Palmer & Turner in 1954, this was one of the city's first skyscrapers. The Bank of China was also the first building to be centrally air-conditioned. Palmer & Turner, formed in Shanghai in 1882, also opened offices in Hong Kong and Johor Bahru before coming to Singapore in the 1940s. This classical Modern building with masonry-like (stone-like) surfaces, is reminiscent of some of the Bank of China's other buildings, as well as some of America's

first skyscrapers. It is also styled similarly to some other established banks of that time, with its Chinese details in stone and bronze. It's now dwarfed by its much taller extension, which has been execute in a clumsy, unsuccessful pastiche.

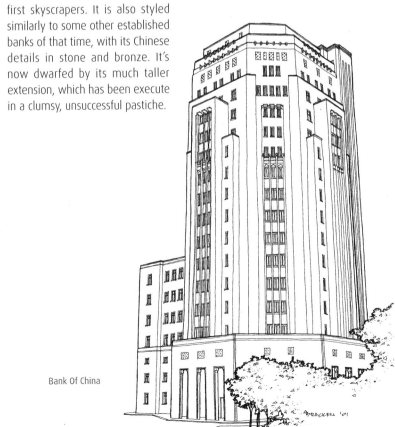

Bank Of China

Boat Quay

## UOB Plaza. . . .

Continue along the waterfront, and the UOB Plaza will be on your left. Its two towers are linked by a pleasant plaza which contains a limited edition sculpture by Salvador Dali called *Homage to Newton*. There is a Chinese restaurant on the 60th floor that affords excellent views of the city. The original octagonal tower by Architects Team 3 was significantly altered in the early 1990s by Kenzo Tange (in conjunction with Architects 61) to match his newer tower (one of the three tallest on the island, standing at 280 metres.

UOB, or the United Overseas Bank, was originally named the United Chinese Bank (UCB), when it was founded on 6 August 1935 by Sarawak-born Datuk Wee Kheng Chiang and his friends. Business was conducted out of the three-storeyed Bonham Building. UCB changed its name in 1965. Having expanded, the bank needed a new building. Bonham Building was demolished and a 30-storeyed UOB Building built and officially opened on 19 October 1974 in its place. The two towers were officially opened in 1995. UOB Plaza was marked as an historic site on 15 October 1999.

**UOB Plaza 1 Si Chuan Dou Hua Restaurant**
60th floor, UOB Plaza 1. 80 Raffles Place. Tel: 6535 6006

## Boat Quay. . . .

Continue past UOB Plaza, and you will come to Boat Quay's row of small-scale shophouses. In the 1860s, most of Singapore's shipping businesses was transacted here. If you were to visit Boat Quay in 1865, you might see as many as 150 boats moored here, and you would have been able to trade in anything from rubber, tin, steel, silk, porcelain and rice, to opium, spices and coffee. This area had various names. The Chinese called it Bu Ye Tian, meaning "place of ceaseless activity". Many of the buildings here were built in the 1920s and 1930s and used as shipping offices, supply shops and warehouses. Boat Quay was designated as a conservation area in 1989.

Boat Quay is now home to more than 35 bars and restaurants, most of which have tables set at the water's edge. It can be a bit loud, but if you want a feel of the area, stop for a quick drink.

## Elgin Bridge. . . .

Follow Boat Quay with the river on your right until you reach your first bridge. This is where the very first bridge in Singapore was built in 1819, linking North Bridge Rd and South Bridge Rd. The present Elgin Bridge was built in 1926, and is the fifth on this site. It takes its name from the fourth bridge (of 1862), an iron import from India which honoured Lord Elgin, Governor-General of India. Its high arches, despite being concrete, are rather graceful, linking the Chinese community on the south side of the river to the Indian merchants on the north side. The cast-iron lamps on either side of the bridge were the work of Rodolfo Nolli, who also designed the bank doors of the Bank of China.

> **Did You Know?**
> The bridges across the Singapore River were all originally built too low and boats couldn't pass under them at high tide.

## MITA Building. . . .

Cross the Elgin Bridge and turn left along North Boat Quay, and you will see the MITA Building at the junction of Hill St and River Valley Rd. This is an imposing, six-storeyed corner building done in an Italianate neoclassical style. Built in 1934 by the Public Works Department as a police station (with barracks for the officers' families) on the site of Singapore's first gaol, it was the largest government building of its day. With its corbelled loggias, it seems almost Florentine in its position overlooking the Singapore River. The police moved out in 1980 and, after restoration in 1999, it now houses the Ministry of Information and the Arts (MITA) and a number of art galleries. Its window frames and shutters have been painted a rainbow range of colours.

Clarke Quay

# Clarke Quay. . . .

Follow the North Boat Quay pedestrian route until you reach Clarke Quay. The junction of the pedestrianised Read St and Clarke St forms a pleasant square. This used to be an area of small godowns. The simple architectural character of these buildings creates quite an attractive streetscape. The godowns on the corner of Read St and North Boat Quay are particularly handsome. Built in the 1860s, they are the oldest remaining godowns in the city. The Satay Club moved here from the Esplanade in the 1990s to make way for the Nicoll Highway extension. Slightly quieter than Boat Quay, some 60 godowns and shophouses have been converted into about 200 shops, restaurants, bars and entertainment outlets and housed in five main blocks: Merchants' Court, The Foundry, The Cannery, Shophouse Row and Traders' Market.

## Singapore Tyler Print Institute. . . .

Continue along the riverside promenade until you come to Caseen St, at the right hand corner of which is the Singapore Tyler Print Institute. This is the Singapore branch of this nonprofit organisation, dedicated to education, the advancement of print- and paper-making, and the creative development of artists. Housed in a nicely restored two-storey godown, its light and airy galleries house a variety of changing exhibitions, as well as a workshop.

**Singapore Tyler Print Institute**
41 Robertson Quay. Tel: 6336 3663
http://www.stpi.com.sg
Open 9:30am to 8pm, Tue-Sat and 1pm to 5pm, Sun-Mon
Admission: Free

## Gallery Hotel. . . .

Continue along the river until you come to Nanson Rd and turn right. The Gallery Hotel will be on your left. This startling and colourful building, completed in 2000, was designed by William Lim Associates and Tangguanbee Architects. It is Singapore's first HIP (Highly Individual Places) hotel. Other HIP hotels around the world have been designed by designers such as Starck, Conran and Hempel. The building consists of a number of different blocks, each with a quite startlingly different appearance. The most arresting is the tower with the almost randomly-placed looking colourful windows overlooking Mohamed Sultan Road.

Gallery Hotel

**Gallery Hotel**
76 Robertson Quay
Tel: 6849 8686.
http://www.galleryhotel.com.sg
general@galleryhotel.com.sg

# Mohamed Sultan Road. . . .
Follow Nanson Road and turn right onto Mohamed Sultan Road. In the 1890s, some of the finest terraced houses in the city were built in the area of River Valley Rd, Kim Yam Rd, Mohamed Sultan Rd and Tong Watt Rd (as well as Emerald Hill Rd, Cuppage Rd and Koek Rd). By the late 1990s, Mohamed Sultan Rd consisted only of a row of decrepit shophouses. These have now been transformed into a Mecca for drinking and partying, one of *the* nightspots to see and be seen in Singapore.

# Hong San See Temple. . . .
Continue along Mohamed Sultan Rd, and you will see the Hong San See Temple on your left. It is a syncretic temple, which means it embraces paganism, Confucianism, Buddhism and Taoism. This also used to be a gathering place for Chinese immigrants from the Fujian province in China. First established in 1829 on Tras St, it was demolished when the government required the land. This new temple was built on a hilltop overlooking Mohamed Sultan Rd between 1908 and 1913 and is similar to the other one-storeyed temples on Telok Ayer St and Magazine Rd. It's also a good example of the open-courtyard-plan type with its stone columns and half-hipped, half-gabled roof. Its wooden artefacts and elaborate carvings were imported from China.

UE Square

# UE Square. . . .

Cross Mohamed Sultan Road and turn left onto Unity St. Taking up almost the entire block between River Valley Rd, Unity St, Mohamed Sultan Rd and Clemenceau Ave, is UE Square, an 18-storeyed office, apartment and shopping complex. The building was designed by Kenzo Tange, and takes its name from the Singaporean engineering firm, United Engineers Limited. This company has also done engineering work on some other important buildings in the city, including Lau Pa Sat and the Supreme Court. Built in 1998, UE Square's residential towers have rather severe lines, a contrast to the curved elevations along Unity St, which are attractive and well-scaled. UE Square is home to a number of restaurants and bars which have spilled over from the neighbouring Mohamed Sultan Rd. Continue down Unity Street, and turn left at Clemenceau Ave. Cross the junction of Clemenceau Ave and River Valley Rd, and you would have reached the edge of Fort Canning Park.

*Link to the Fort Canning Park walk: Take the first staircase up on your right.*

# Fort Canning Park

**Nearest MRT: Dhoby Ghaut**
**Approximate walking time: 30 minutes**

## Museum District

Known as *Bukit Larangan* or the Forbidden Hill when Raffles landed in 1819, Fort Canning was home to Malay royalty in the 14th century and was considered by some to be sacred, and hence, forbidden, ground. Today, Fort Canning Park is beautifully landscaped and contains some interesting sites and buildings. It also commands some excellent views of the city centre. It is surrounded by a number of important museums, including the Singapore History Museum, the Asian Civilisations Museum and the Singapore Philatelic Museum. Some architecturally important buildings are also found here, notably the elegant little Armenian Church and the unusual SCCCI Building.

# THE WALK

See detailed map on page 48

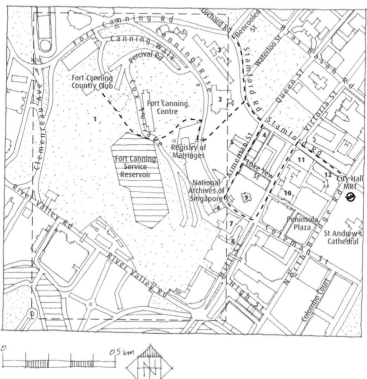

## KEY

1. Fort Canning Park
2. National Library (Former)
3. Singapore History Museum
4. MPH Building
5. Asian Civilisations Museum, Armenian St.
6. Singapore Philatelic Museum
7. Masonic Lodge
8. Central Fire Station
9. Armenian Church
10. Singapore Chinese Chamber of
    Commerce & Industry Building (SCCCI Building)
11. Stamford House
12. Capitol Building

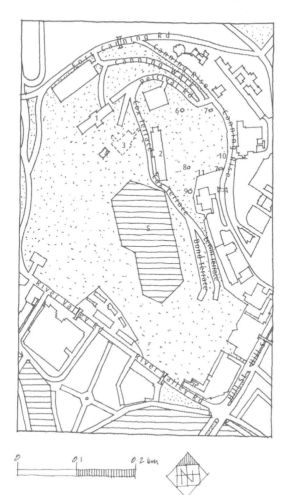

## Key: Fort Canning Park

1. Fort Canning Country Club
2. Fort Canning Centre
3. Battle Box
4. Fort Gate
5. Reservoir
6. Asean Sculpture Garden
7. Gothic Gate
8. Cupolas
9. Keramat Iskandar Shah
10. Spice Garden (former)
11. Headstones

# Fort Canning Park. . . .

If you are walking from Dhoby Ghaut MRT, leave the station and follow the signs for Fort Canning Park.

Before Raffles, Fort Canning was known as Forbidden Hill. In 1833, Raffles built a house and set up Singapore's first botanical gardens on its premises. His bungalow served as the Government House for succeeding governors until 1857 when the land for the Istana was bought. Government House was later demolished, and a military fort was built in its place. The fort was named in honour of Lord Canning, the first Viceroy of India.

Raffles also established a Christian cemetery on the hill. Not much remains of this but some fine neoclassical monuments (possibly by Irish architect G.D. Coleman), the original two Gothic gateways (from 1846), the gateway of the fort and a guardhouse. The last Malay ruler of Singapore, Sultan Iskandar Shah, is also said to be buried here. There's a *keramat* (shrine) to him on the east side of the hill, which is revered as a holy place.

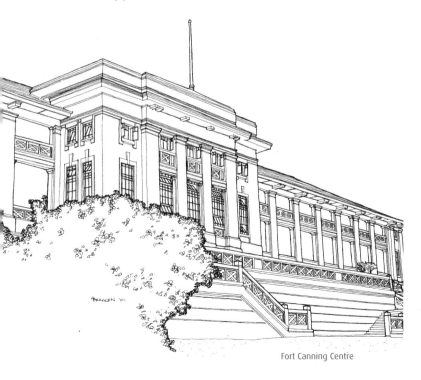

Fort Canning Centre

This hill was also the location of the Spice Garden, the original Botanic Gardens, where Raffles experimented with the cultivation of spices. (Spice in early 19th century trade was more valuable than gold.) Cloves and cinnamon were planted here.

Fort Canning Centre, a restored military barracks, is now a cultural venue for performing arts companies. The former Singapore Command and Staff College has been converted into the Fort Canning Country Club. The grounds, renamed Fort Canning Park in 1981, provides some excellent views of the city centre.

**Fort Canning Park & Centre • Cox Terrace • Fort Canning Park**
51 Canning Rise
Tel: 6332 1200 (for information on tours, exhibitions and the hiring of grounds and facilities).
Offices open from 8:30am to 5 pm, Mon–Fri and 8:30am to 1 pm, Sat
Admission: Free
Park is lit between 7pm and 7am daily

**Note: Sir Thomas Stamford Raffles (1781–1826)**
The only son of a merchant captain, Raffles was born mid-Atlantic on his father's ship in 1781. At 14, he started working as a clerk for the East India Company, and in 1805 he was posted as an assistant secretary to the government in Penang. Appointed lieutenant governor of Java from 1811–1816, Raffles was the only colonial official able to speak Malay. He fought tirelessly to suppress piracy and slavery (even though it was said that he used slaves on his own plantations) and was also a passionate advocate of free trade, having seen the detrimental effects of the Dutch trade monopoly on the region. When Java was given back to the Dutch in 1818, Raffles was appointed lieutenant governor of Bencoolen (now Bengkulu) in Sumatra, Indonesia. While he was there, he came to realise that Britain increasingly needed a power base on the China trade route. He obtained the Governor-General of India's permission to look for a suitable location at the tip of the Malay Peninsula.

Raffles landed at Singapore in January 1819 after discovering that the Dutch had already reestablished themselves on Bintan. He then quickly arranged with the *temenggong* (Malay chief) to set up a trading post. Raffles visited Singapore in 1822–23, by which time the port was booming and was home to 10,000 people. Before leaving, he drew up a constitution, a street plan (over which he had a quarrel with the Resident, Major W. Farquhar, who later claimed to have founded the city himself), and established the Raffles Institution. Raffles returned to England in 1824 when his health began to deteriorate. In London, he assisted with the founding of the London Zoo. Raffles died the day before his 45th birthday of a suspected brain tumor in 1826. Eight years later, thanks to the efforts of his second wife, Lady Sophia Raffles, a commemorative statue of him was placed in Westminster Abbey in London.

# National Library (Former). . . .

Leave Fort Canning Park via the pedestrian underpass beside the Registry of Marriages. It will take you into the carpark of the National Library. This is a monumental red-brick building soon to be replaced by a new library building by T.R. Hamzah & Yeang (in association with Swan & Maclaren) on Victoria St in 2005. The present site will become part of the new campus of the Singapore Management University.

**National Library**
91 Stamford Rd. http://www.nlb.gov.sg
The library has been permanently closed from 1 April 2004

# Singapore History Museum. . . .

With the National Library behind you, turn left and follow the pedestrian path along Stamford Rd toward the Singapore History Museum. The Raffles Library and Museum was opened in 1887, having been previously housed in the Raffles Institution. The building was designed by Major H.E. McCallum and has been sympathetically extended twice, the simple white paintwork enhancing its neoclassical character.

This domed building was renamed the National Museum in 1960 and then the Singapore History Museum. The 117-year old museum is closed for extensive redevelopment until 2006. Temporary premises for the museum can be found at Riverside Point at Merchant Road.

> **Did You Know?**
> The Singapore History Museum is home to the recently rediscovered portrait of early 20th century Governor Sir Frank Swettenham by Sir John Singer Sargent. A particularly handsome painting, this had been hidden away for years before anyone realised how valuable it was.

**Singapore History Museum (Riverside Point)**
30 Merchant Rd. Tel: 6332 5642. http://www.museum.org.sg/SHM
Open from 9am to 7pm, Tue–Sun and 1pm to 7pm, Mon
Late night opening till 9pm on Friday
Admission: Adult S$2, students (above 6 years) and senior citizens (over 60) S$1. Free admission after 7pm on Friday
Free guided tours are available in English, Japanese, and Mandarin.
Check the museum website or call the museum for tour times.

# MPH Building. . . .

Coming out of the Singapore History Museum, turn right and retrace your steps past the National Library on your right. At the corner of Stamford Rd and Armenian St is the MPH Building. Formerly home to MPH Bookstore, this is a good piece of commercial street architecture by Swan & Maclaren. Built in 1908, its elaborately modelled three-storeyed façade is typically Edwardian. It also wouldn't look out of place in central London.

Asian Civilisations Museum,
Armenian St

# Asian Civilisations Museum, Armenian St . . . .

Farther down Armenian St, on the opposite side of the road from MPH, is the Asian Civilisations Museum. Originally built by Swan & Maclaren in 1910 to house the Tao Nan School, it was one of several schools originally built in this area. Saved from demolition — unlike the Raffles Girls' School and the Raffles Institution — this elegantly symmetrical, neoclassical building was the first home of the Asian Civilisations Museum before the museum expanded to Empress Place. The main exhibition here is on Peranakan culture. Next door is the Substation, a small venue for arts performances and exhibitions housed in a blue three-storeyed art deco brick building.

### Asian Civilisations Museum, Armenian St
39 Armenian St. Tel: 6332 3015
http://www.museum.org.sg/ACM/acm.shtml
Open from 9am to 7pm, Tue–Sun and 1pm to 7pm, Mon
Late night opening till 9pm on Friday
Admission: Adult S\$3, students (above 6 years) and senior citizens (over 60) S\$1.50. Free admission after 7pm on Friday
Free guided tours are available in English and Japanese.
Check the museum website or call the museum for tour times.

### The Substation
45 Armenian St. Tel: 6337 7535
http://www.substation.org

# Singapore Philatelic Museum. . . .

Continue to the end of Armenian St to find the Singapore Philatelic Museum, sandwiched between the Singapore Archives on its right and the Masonic Lodge on its left. Built around 1895 and formerly known as the Methodist Book Room building, it's nicely scaled and well proportioned. Though rather unexceptional architecturally, it is surprisingly charming, perhaps because it looks like it belongs to different times. It became the Singapore Philatelic Museum in 1995 and is Southeast Asia's only philatelic museum.

**Singapore Philatelic Museum**
23B Coleman St. Tel: 6433 7347. http://www.spm.org.sg
Open from 9am to 7pm, Tue–Sun and 1pm to 7pm, Mon
Admission: Adult S$2, students (above 6 years) and
senior citizens (over 60) S$1

# Masonic Lodge. . . .

Next to the Singapore Philatelic Museum is the Masonic Lodge. This elegant, symmetrical two-storeyed building was designed by D.M. Craik in 1879. Although it has been altered and extended three times, it still retains its original shape and character. The use of neoclassical details is restrained. Originally, the Masonic Lodge was located in the house of Thomas Church on the Esplanade. In the 1870s, before Beach Rd fell out of fashion with the Europeans, the Masons used to meet in a house there.

Masonic Lodge

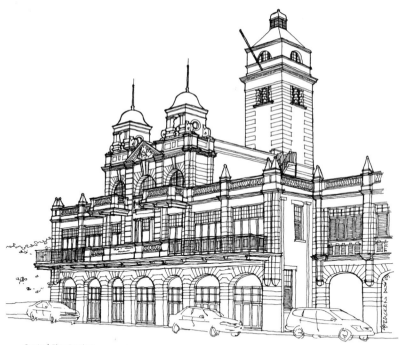

Central Fire Station

## Central Fire Station. . . .

**Did You Know?**
This building's tower was not designed as a lookout post, but for drying the fire-hoses after use to prevent them from rotting.

At the corner where Coleman St meets Hill St, you will see the Central Fire Station. Built in 1909 by the Municipal Council of Singapore, the Central Fire Station was the first fully equipped fire station on the island. The "blood and bandage" elevation treatment (bands of white plaster alternating with red brick) is typically Edwardian and makes a pleasant change from the relentless white-on-white neoclassicism found throughout the rest of the original city centre. During World War II, the building was painted camouflage colours.

## Armenian Church. . . .

**Did You Know?**
Agnes Joaquim, discoverer of Singapore's national flower, is buried here. This Armenian lady came across the Vanda Miss Joaquim orchid in the extensive grounds of her residence at 2 Narcis Rd, off Tanjong Pagar, in 1893.

Beside the Central Fire Station and overlooking Hill St are the lush landscaped grounds of the Armenian Church. Dedicated to St Gregory the Illuminator, the first monk of the Armenian Church, this gem of a building was designed by G.D. Coleman and built in 1835. It was funded by the small Armenian community and merchants from various backgrounds. The tower and spire are not part of the original design but were added by an English architect, Maddock, in 1847, when the traditional Armenian-style dome and bell turret were removed. An east portico was added around the existing chancel, and the main west portico was widened. The parsonage, which sits in the same grounds, is also a fine building.

## Singapore Chinese Chamber of Commerce & Industry Building. . . .

Farther along Hill St, with the Armenian Church to your left, you will see the Singapore Chinese Chamber of Commerce & Industry Building on your right. Built in 1964 by Chung Swee Poey & Sons, this building is an odd, but not unpleasant, mix of East and West, not dissimilar in style to the later Marriott (formerly Dynasty) Hotel on Orchard Rd. Its red portals, glazed tiles, carved beams, painted columns and the murals on each side of the gate resemble a traditional Chinese palace. The large lions at the entrance were imported from China. The Chinese Chamber of Commerce was officially inaugurated in 1906.

SCCCI Building

BRACKEN '01

Fort Canning

## Stamford House. . . .

Walking in the same direction, on the right where Hill St meets Stamford Rd, you will find Stamford House. Originally built in 1904 as the Oranje Hotel, it was used by the Japanese during their occupation. Designed by R.A.J. Bidwell of Swan & Maclaren (who was also responsible for the Raffles and Goodwood Park Hotels), it was refurbished when it changed hands in the mid-1960s and was renamed Stamford House. This three-storeyed building was constructed in the Venetian renaissance style.

## Capitol Building. . . .

Turn right onto Stamford Rd and follow it until you come to the Capitol Building, located at the corner of Stamford Rd and North Bridge Rd. Typical of the work of the firm of Keys & Dowdeswell, this handsome, if rather heavily detailed, neoclassical building dates from 1930. Capitol Building's Stamford Rd façade is a particularly fine piece of street architecture and turns the corner onto North Bridge Rd so well that it seems to have emboldened the architects of the MRT headquarters, on the opposite side of Stamford Rd, to attempt something similar.

*Link to the Padang walk: Cross North Bridge Rd and enter the grounds of St Andrew's Cathedral.*

Capitol Building

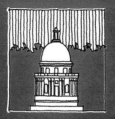

# The Padang

**Nearest MRT: City Hall**
**Approximate walking time: 25 minutes**

## Government Enclave

Once known as the Plain, the Padang (Malay for "playing field")
was originally bordered on the south by the sea. After land
reclamation, it is now about 1 kilometre (0.6 miles) inland.
It was here that the Japanese herded Singapore's Caucasian residents
before marching them to Changi for internment for the duration of
the Japanese Occupation. Now the site of important sporting events
and the focal point of the National Day Parades, it is bordered by
some of the city's most important buildings, notably the City Hall and
the Supreme Court.

# THE WALK

See detailed map on page 63

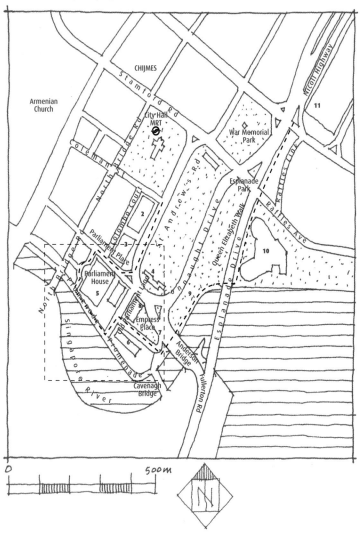

# KEY

The Padang

# St Andrew's Cathedral. . . .

> **Did You Know?**
> The four paths converging on the cathedral form the Cross of St Andrew.

This is the first church you will see when you emerge from City Hall MRT. This Anglican cathedral is the third building to be erected here. G.D. Coleman's original Palladian church of St Andrew was built in 1836. This building, in the English-Gothic style, probably based on 13th century Netley Abbey in England, was built by Indian convict labour. Designed by Lieutenant-Colonel Ronald MacPherson, its first service was held in 1861, and it was consecrated as a cathedral in 1870. Like many other churches in the city, St Andrew's Cathedral was used as an emergency hospital during the Japanese invasion.

# City Hall. . . .

Leave St Andrew's Cathedral via the St Andrew's Rd exit facing the Padang. Cross Coleman St, and City Hall will be the first building on your right. Municipal Architect A. Gordon and Assistant Architect F.D. Meadows designed this dull neoclassical building around 1929. Originally known as the Municipal Building, it replaced some beautiful houses, most likely built by G.D. Coleman around 1830. The Japanese general Seishiro Itagaki surrendered to Lord Mountbatten on these steps on 12 September 1945. Renamed City Hall in 1951, it was here that Lee Kuan Yew declared Singapore's independence on 9 August 1965. Access to its premises is restricted.

**Note: Lee Kuan Yew**

Lee Kuan Yew is widely regarded as the father of modern Singapore. A lawyer turned politician, Lee was instrumental in turning Singapore from a backwater colonial outpost with appalling slums and rampant race riots into an international byword for excellence and efficiency. To some in the West, his authoritarian style, largely based on Confucian ethics, especially respect for one's elders, is said to have turned Singaporeans into timid citizens. While recognizing that his policies have worked wonders, some Westerners complain that Lee's achievements have resulted in an antiseptic and arid society with little room for individual creativity or imagination. While Singapore is not Paris or New York, one look at its thriving arts scene, as well as the robust popular culture catering for every imaginable taste, contradicts this view.

Lee Kuan Yew was born into an English-speaking Hakka Chinese family on 16 September 1923. Revealing a touchingly human side, Lee and his wife, Kwa Geok Choo, married each other secretly while they were still undergraduates at Cambridge University. Back in Singapore, they set up the law firm, Lee and Lee. Lee served as Singapore's prime minister from 1959 to 1990 and is currently the senior minister.

# Supreme Court. . . .

Walking down St Andrew's Rd, the next building on your right is the Supreme Court, originally the Grand Hotel de l'Europe, the last of four hotels on this site. This hotel was closed in 1932 to make way for the Supreme Court. This badly proportioned courthouse, by F.D. Ward of the Public Works Department, was completed in 1939, making it the last colonial neoclassical building built in Singapore. The pediment sculpture shows an allegory of justice, executed by a team of Italian craftsmen, headed by Milanese Rudolpho Nolli, who had also worked on the King of Siam's (now Thailand's) throne hall.

**Supreme Court Multimedia Gallery**
1 St Andrew's Rd
Open from 8:30am to 5 pm, Mon–Fri
and 8:30am to 1 pm, Sat
Admission: Free

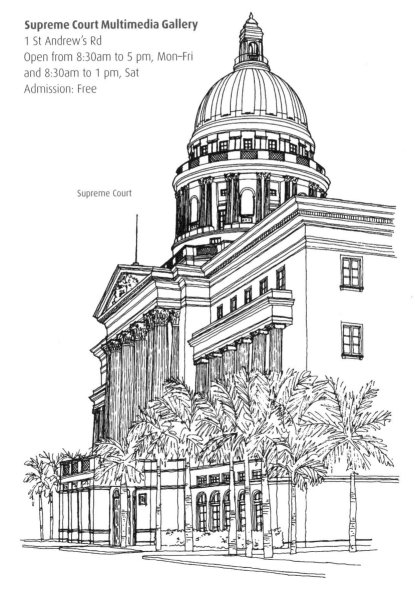

Supreme Court

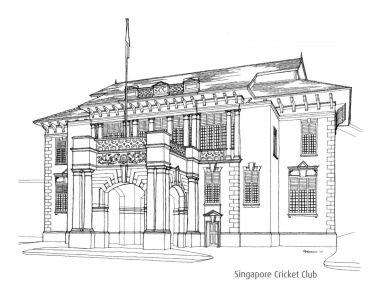

Singapore Cricket Club

# Singapore Cricket Club. . . .

At one end of the Padang sits a nicely scaled late Victorian building — the Singapore Cricket Club. Cricket has been played on the Padang since the 1830s. Founded in 1852, the club's first building was built around the 1860s. A second pavilion was built in 1877 and a third, by Swan & Maclaren (who won an architectural competition for its design), in 1884. Wings and a new verandah facing the Padang were added in the early 1920s. Major W. Farquhar (the first Resident of Singapore) built a temporary house here.

**Did You Know?**
All the buildings between the Padang and the river were going to be knocked down in the 1940s to make way for F.D. Ward's plan for a new government enclave. This included the Singapore Cricket Club, Parliament House and the Victoria Concert Hall & Theatre. Fortunately, World War II intervened.

# Parliament Complex. . . .

### A. The Arts House (formerly known as Old Parliament House)

At the end of St Andrew's Rd you will see the two buildings that form The Arts House. A small bronze statue of an elephant fronts the building. This was supposed to be the home of J.A. Maxwell, but before he had the chance to live here, the government took it over for use as a courthouse. Built in 1827 by G.D. Coleman, it is the oldest government building on the island. The Legislative Assembly occupied it in 1954, and it was the Parliament House from 1965 to 1999. A long extension was added in 1875 by J.F.A. McNair (Colonial Architect of the Public Works Department), and there were further extensions and remodelling over the years. Between 1999 and 2004, the building underwent redevelopment. Its façade was preserved, and its interior was renovated to accommodate performing arts spaces, such as a film theatrette and Black Box space. Today The Arts House is Singapore's newest space for the performing arts.

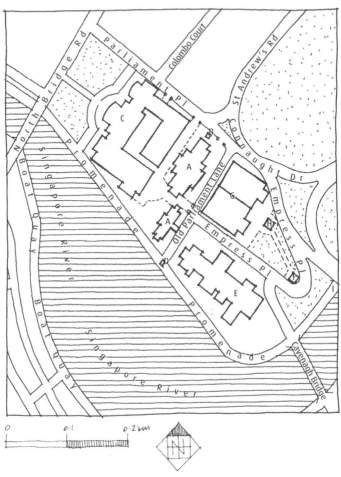

## Key: Parliament Complex

A. The Arts House
B. Bronze elephant
C. Parliament House
D. Raffles' Landing Site
E. Asian Civilisations Museum, Empress Place
F. Dalhousie Memorial
G. Victoria Concert Hall & Theatre
H. Raffles' statue
I. Underpass to the Esplanade

The Padang

## B. Bronze Elephant

The bronze statue of an elephant in front of The Arts House was a gift from King Chulalongkorn of Siam (now Thailand) to commemorate his visit to Singapore in 1871. Singapore was the first foreign country to be visited by a Siamese monarch.

## C. Parliament House

Turning right onto Parliament Place from St Andrew's Rd, you will see the new Parliament House on your left. The front of Parliament House is farther down, facing North Bridge Rd. Built by the Public Works Department and completed in 1999, the relative plainness of this symmetrical building acts as a foil to its neoclassical neighbours. It's a rather bland building, with vaguely fascist overtones, which all but ignores its riverside context.

### Parliament House

1 Parliament Place. Tel: 6332 6666. http://www.gov.sg/parliament
(Public entrance on Parliament Place)
Tours are available by appointment only. To enter the Strangers' Gallery when Parliament is in session, Singaporeans require their I.C. and non-Singaporeans, their passport, in exchange for admissions passes.

## D. Raffles' Landing Site

Follow the riverside promenade, and you will find Singapore's second statue of Raffles, sculptored by Thomas Woolner. Made in 1972 from plaster casts of the original statue, this marks what is thought to be Raffles' landing site. The first statue, cast in bronze in 1887, was originally unveiled on the Padang but was moved to its current location in front of the Victoria Concert Hall & Theatre in 1919.

# Asian Civilisations Museum, Empress Place. . . .

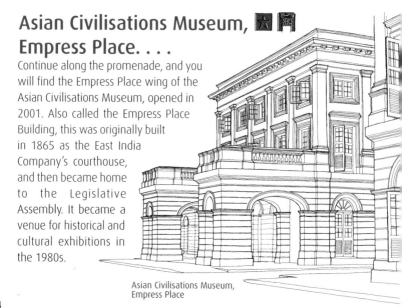

Continue along the promenade, and you will find the Empress Place wing of the Asian Civilisations Museum, opened in 2001. Also called the Empress Place Building, this was originally built in 1865 as the East India Company's courthouse, and then became home to the Legislative Assembly. It became a venue for historical and cultural exhibitions in the 1980s.

Asian Civilisations Museum, Empress Place

### Asian Civilisations Museum, Empress Place

1 Empress Place. Tel: 6332 7798
http://www.museum.org.sg/ACM/acm.shtml
Open from 9am to 7pm, Tue–Sun and 1pm to 7pm, Mon
Late night opening till 9pm on Friday
Admission: Adult S$5, students (above 6 years) and senior citizens
(over 60) S$2.50. Free admission after 7pm on Friday
Free guided tours are available in English, Japanese and Mandarin.
Check the museum website or call the museum for tour times.

### Note: George Drumgoole Coleman

Born in Ireland in 1794, G.D. Coleman worked as an architect in Calcutta in 1815 and was later employed by Raffles, in 1820, as a town planning consultant in Batavia (now Jakarta). He moved to Singapore in 1826 to take up the position of Town Surveyor, and was also Superintendent of Public Works. There is no record of where he was trained, though he was well-versed in the neoclassical architecture of the day, most notably the Palladian style which he skillfully adapted to suit the tropical climate — Doric columns, high ceilings, open floor plans and wide verandahs to provide relief from the heat. Coleman was also responsible for the drainage of the marshes on either side of the Singapore River and the layout of the road network, still evident in the city. The Armenian Church, Caldwell House (in Chijmes) and Maxwell House were privately commissioned by Coleman. He is also thought to have been involved in designing the Istana Kampong Gelam. The house he designed for himself — № 3 Coleman St — was built along a road named in his honour. A simple two-storeyed brick house in a classical design, it was demolished in 1969 to make way for the Peninsula Hotel.

# Dalhousie Memorial. . . .

Beyond the museum, you will find a landscaped park that contains another statue of Raffles as well as the Dalhousie Memorial. Acting as a focal point for Empress Place, the Dalhousie Memorial was built in 1850 and designed by J.T. Thompson, Government Surveyor. It was moved twice before coming to its present position in 1891. It was built to commemorate the second visit to Singapore of the Governor-General of India, the Marquess of Dalhousie, and serves as a reminder of the benefits of free trade. Some say it was probably inspired by Cleopatra's Needle on the Thames Embankment in London.

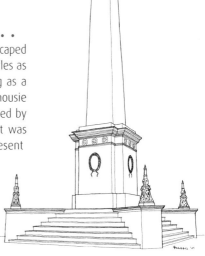

Dalhousie Memorial

## Victoria Concert Hall & Theatre. . . .

Serving as abackdrop to the Dalhousie Memorial is the Victoria Concert Hall & Theatre. Designed by John Bennett and built between 1856 and 1862 to commemorate Queen Victoria, this was Singapore's Town Hall until 1893. The second Hall (originally called Memorial Hall, now the Concert Hall) and the tower were added in the same architectural style by R.A.J. Bidwell of Swan & Maclaren in 1905. The Concert Hall was renovated and airconditioned in the early 1950s and further improved in the late 1970s when a gallery was added. It is now home to the Singapore Symphony Orchestra, which was formed in 1978.

**Victoria Concert Hall & Theatre**
9 and 11 Empress Place. Tel: 6333 0041. http://www.vch.org.sg or Singapore Symphony Orchestra http://www. sso.org.sg
Tickets for most concerts and events in Singapore can be booked through:

**TICKET CHARGE**   Tel: 6296 2929. http://www.ticketcharge.com.sg
**SISTIC**   Tel: 6348 5555. http://www.sistic.com.sg

## The Esplanade. . . .

Cross the underpass located near the Dalhousie Memorial along the Promenade to reach the Esplanade, one of Singapore's oldest parks. The elongated park located along Connaught Dr contains three historical landmarks:

### A. Lim Bo Seng Memorial

This is a pagoda-like concrete memorial to a national World War II hero and martyr, unveiled in 1954. It has Italian marble facing, a bronze roof and four bronze lions (imported from Hong Kong). Lim Bo Seng was part of the underground resistance leading the Chinese civil defence in Singapore. In 1943, he was leading the guerillas of Force 136 in Perak when he was captured by the Japanese and tortured to death. He was only 34 years old.

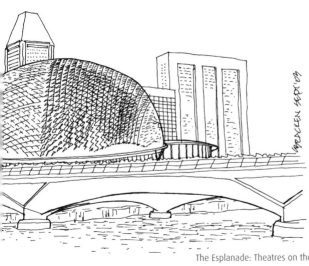

The Esplanade: Theatres on the Bay

### B. Cenotaph

Designed by Denis Santry of Swan & Maclaren, the Cenotaph is a memorial to the 124 Singaporean men who died in World War I. It is presumed to have been modelled on the English architect Sir Edwin Lutyens's Cenotaph in Whitehall, London. Its foundation stone was laid by the Governor of the Straits Settlements, Sir Lawrence Guillemard, in the presence of the French Premier George Clemenceau and General Officer Major-General Sir D.H. Ridout in 1920.

### C. Tan Kim Seng Fountain

This fountain was named after the philanthropist who donated $13,000 towards Singapore's first waterworks in 1857. (It was said that more of this money went toward the building of the fountain than the waterworks.) Originally unveiled at Fullerton Square in 1882, it was relocated to the Esplanade in 1925. In 1862, Tan Kim Seng owned 11.6 sq km (2,859 acres) of land, half the area between Telok Blangah and Clementi Rd, and probably the largest parcel of land ever owned by a single individual in Singapore.

# The Esplanade: Theatres on the Bay. . . .

Continue along Queen Elizabeth Walk and then turn right under the Esplanade Drive, and you will see the Theatres on the Bay ahead of you. Nicknamed 'the durians' by locals these aggressively detailed blobs house a number of state-of-the-art cultural facilities as well as a host of shops and restaurants. Designed by DP Architects in association with Michael Wilford and Partners of London, it was completed in 2002.

### The Esplanade: Theatres on the Bay

1 Esplanade Dr. Tel: 6828 8377. http://www.esplanade.com
Tickets can be purchased through SISTIC. Guided Tours available at S$8 (adults) and S$5 (child aged 12 and below).

The Padang

## Suntec City. . . .

Suntec City

Farther down Esplanade Dr, at the junction of Esplanade Dr and Raffles Blvd, is Suntec City. Designed in 1994 by D.P. Architects in association with Tsao & McKown, it's the largest privately owned commercial development in Singapore. It comprises of a 18-storeyed office building, four 45-storeyed office towers and a 3-storeyed shopping and entertainment complex, featuring the world's largest fountain. Designed to obey the precepts of feng shui, the towers represent an open hand and the fountain plaza, a gold ring (water being a symbol of wealth) resting on its palm. D.P. Architects's 41-storeyed Millenia Tower (in association with Kevin Roach, John Dinkeloo and Associates) and the starkly postmodern Millenia Walk (in association with Philip Johnson and John Burgee Architects) adjoining the Suntec Complex, are complementary in their architectural expression.

*Link to the Bras Basah Road walk: Cross Nicoll Highway with your back to either Suntec City or One Raffles Link and enter the War Memorial Park.*

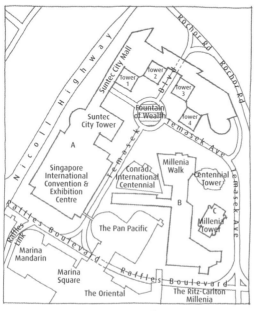

### Key: Suntec City

A. Suntec City
B. Millenia Walk
C. Millenia Tower

# Bras Basah Road

**Nearest MRT: City Hall**
**Approximate walking time: 30 minutes**

## Cultural District

Bras Basah Rd, which means "wet rice" in Malay, derives its name from the practice of drying wet rice on the banks of the nearby now culverted Stamford Canal. There used to be a convict station located nearby which housed Indian prisoners, many of whom were forced to labour on some of Singapore's most famous buildings, including St Andrew's Cathedral. In the middle of the 19th century, Bras Basah Rd was home to the best selection of secondhand bookshops in the city and a favourite haunt of students. It is fitting that the Singapore Management University has planned to build its new campus here.

# THE WALK

See detailed map on page 75

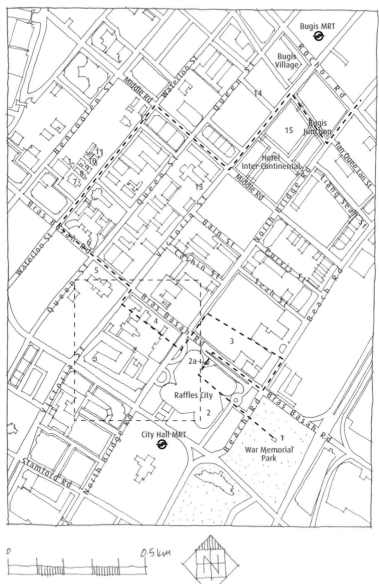

# KEY

1. War Memorial Park
2. Raffles City (2a Raffles Institution Monument)
3. Raffles Hotel
4. Chijmes
5. Cathedral of the Good Shepherd
6. Singapore Art Museum
7. Maghain Aboth Synagogue
8. Action Theatre
9. Singapore Calligraphy Centre
10. Young Musicians' Society
11. Dance Ensemble Singapore
12. Sculpture Square
13. St Joseph's Church
14. New Bugis St
15. Bugis Junction

# War Memorial Park. . . .

After exiting the City Hall MRT, walk in the direction of Beach Rd. You will come to a park facing Raffles City on its eastern side. This is the War Memorial Park, where a 67-metre (220-foot) memorial stands. Resembling two pairs of chopsticks, it was built by Swan & Maclaren in 1964 to commemorate the civilians killed during the Japanese Occupation. The four pillars are meant to represent the four races in Singapore: Chinese, Malay, Indian and other races.

# Raffles City. . . .

Cross Beach Rd back toward City Hall MRT and Raffles City. Raffles City is an imposing cluster of towers incorporating Swissôtel The Stamford (one of the tallest hotels in the world); Raffles The Plaza, Singapore; an office tower and the Raffles City Shopping Centre. Designed by I.M. Pei & Partners (in association with Architect 61) it was built in 1985. Being the only tall building in this part of the city, it is rather imposing. Architecturally, it has considerable merit, the shapes are simple but interesting, and the balcony openings give the towers a rhythm. Initially the aluminium cladding caused a great deal of glare but weathering has reduced this over the years. It was built on the site of the Raffles Institution which was the first school in Singapore and was founded by Raffles himself. There's a marked historic site and a small monument to this school outside the Bras Basah Rd exit of the shopping centre.

## Equinox
70th floor, Swissôtel The Stamford
Tel: 64316156 (Reservations)
http://www.equinoxcomplex.com
Excellent views of the city, especially at night.

Raffles City

# Raffles Hotel. . . .

**Did You Know?**
Raffles Hotel wasn't expected to survive because everyone thought it was built on the "wrong" end of the Padang, the fashionable hotels being at its southern end. Ironically, it was Raffles' main rival, the Hotel de l'Europe, that didn't last.

Exit Raffles City via the Bras Basah Rd exit and you will see Raffles Hotel across the road. Raffles Hotel opened on 1 December 1887, but it was the 1899 opening of the main building that marked its transformation into a grand hotel. Designed by R.A.J. Bidwell of Swan & Maclaren in a rather eclectic looking Palladian style, it was extended again in the 1920s. By the 1980s, it was in a state of disrepair and was restored in the early 1990s, when all the insensitive additions and alterations were removed. It was founded by the Armenian Sarkies brothers, who also owned the E&O Hotel in Penang and the Strand Hotel in Rangoon (now Yangon). Its guests include Joseph Conrad, W. Somerset Maugham (who wrote some of his short stories while staying here), Noel Coward and Rudyard Kipling (who seemed to prefer the Hotel de l'Europe, since he advised his friends only to eat at the Raffles). There are a number of restaurants and bars, including the famous Long Bar, birthplace of the Singapore Sling cocktail (in 1915). There's also a shopping complex, a theatre (named after the Jubilee Hall Theatre which was knocked down to make way for the shopping complex) and a small museum.

**Raffles Hotel**
1 Beach Rd. Tel: 6337 1886. http://www.raffleshotel.com

Chijmes

# Chijmes. . . .

Leave Raffles Hotel on the side facing Bras Basah Rd or North Bridge Rd. Cross these roads to get to Chijmes at the opposite junction. This was formerly the site of the girls' schools: Convent of the Holy Infant Jesus and St Nicholas Girls' School, founded in 1854 for fee-paying day-pupils and boarders. Caldwell House, an architectural gem by G.D. Coleman from 1841, was bought by Reverend Beurel in 1852. A series of convent buildings were built between 1855 and 1892, including the delicate French Gothic chapel designed by Father Nain. Swan & Maclaren designed the St Nicholas Girls' School building in 1913 and were responsible for further extensions in 1951. After the school moved to a new location in 1983, the complex fell into disrepair before being turned into an up-market shopping and entertainment centre. A self-contained block of considerable architectural merit and charm, the various buildings, although in different architectural styles, work well together and are clustered around differently shaped courtyards.

# Cathedral of the Good Shepherd. . . .

Cross Victoria St and you will be at the Cathedral of the Good Shepherd. Set in leafy grounds, this fine neoclassical Catholic cathedral was built in 1846 (it became a cathedral in 1888). Architect Dennis McSwinney, formerly a clerk

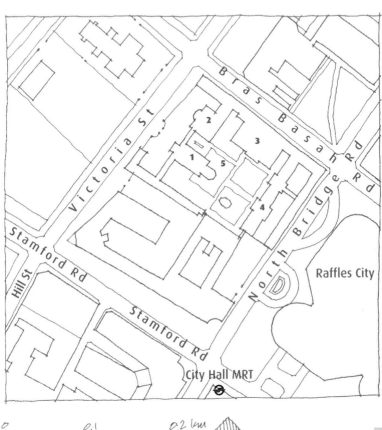

## Key: Chijmes

1. Chijmes Hall
2. Caldwell House
3. East Manor
4. West Manor
5. Fountain Court

to G.D. Coleman, beat J.T. Thompson in the design competition mainly, it seems, because his design was considered less expensive to maintain. Done in a restrained Renaissance style, it has a high timber-decorated ceiling, and its porches are Palladian in style (reminiscent of the work of Coleman). It's regarded as one of the finest buildings in Singapore but has, sadly, been painted a dull beige and brown. It was used as an emergency hospital during the Japanese invasion. The cathedral compound also contains the Archbishop's House, the Resident's Quarters and the Priest's House.

Singapore Art Museum

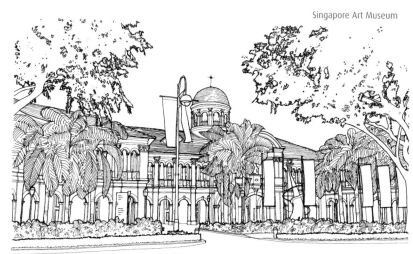

## Singapore Art Museum. . . .

With the Cathedral of the Good Shepherd at your left, walk along Bras Basah Rd, crossing Queen St. To your right will be the Singapore Art Museum. Formerly St Joseph's Institution, it was built in 1867 on the site of the first Catholic chapel in Singapore. The present building was designed by Brother Lothaire, who came to Singapore to set up a Catholic boys' school. Its curved wings were added by another priest-architect, Father Nain, in 1906. Its verandahs have been enclosed with glass and its galleries air-conditioned. The sweeping wings sit in fine relationship to Bras Basah Rd.

**Singapore Art Museum**
71 Bras Basah Rd. Tel: 6332 3222
http://www.museum.org.sg/SAM
Open from 9am to 7pm, Mon–Sun
Late night opening till 9pm on Friday
Admission: Adult S$3, students (above 6 years) and senior citizens (over 60) S$1.50. Free admission after 6pm on Friday
Free guided tours are available in English, Japanese and Mandarin. Check the museum website or call the museum for tour times.

# Maghain Aboth Synagogue. . . .

Keeping the Singapore Art Museum on your right, turn right at Waterloo St. You will spot Maghain Aboth Synagogue on your left — an eclectic Victorian-style building with a spacious, elegant interior. Built in 1878 as the first place of worship for the small but influential Jewish community (before this they had worshipped in a small shop on Synagogue St), it was restored in 2000.

# The Action Theatre. . . .

This theatre is located next door to the synagogue (at 42 Waterloo St) in an attractive, symmetrical two-storeyed bungalow, the first in a row of buildings dedicated to the arts.

**The Action Theatre**
42 Waterloo St. Tel: 6837 0842. http://www.action.org.sg
info@action.org.sg

# Singapore Calligraphy Centre. . . .

Number 48 is a fine neoclassical bungalow, home to the Singapore Calligraphy Centre.

# Young Musicians' Society. . . .

54 Waterloo St, with its highly decorative gable and hallway, is the first in a row of three unusually ornate shophouses, housing the Young Musicians' Society (YMS).

**Young Musicians' Society**
54–58 Waterloo St. Tel: 6332 5813. http://www.yms.org.sg

# Dance Ensemble Singapore. . . .

The dance ensemble occupies № 60, a simple, symmetrical Early Style bungalow.

# Sculpture Square. . . .

At the junction of Waterloo St and Middle Rd stands a tiny one-storeyed Gothic chapel, built in 1870. A sculpture gallery, highlighting Asian talent, can be found here. Its annexe is housed in the neighbouring Early Style bungalow which overlooks a delightful little urban space known as Sculpture Square. It is also the outdoor seating area for an up-market restaurant.

**Sculpture Square Limited**
Contemporary 3-D Art Centre
155 Middle Rd. Tel: 6333 1055
http://www.sculpturesq.com.sg

# St Joseph's Church. . . .

Leaving Waterloo St, turn right onto Middle Rd. Walk down this road, passing Queen St on your right, until you get to Victoria St. Along this street, on your right is St Joseph's Church. Dedicated to San Jose, it was originally built on this site with money bequeathed for that purpose by Father Francisco da Silva Pinto e Maia of Porto, head of the Portuguese Mission, who arrived in 1826. The King of Portugal also contributed to the funds. Replacing a neoclassical building, this present church dates from 1912 and is executed in a light Gothic stye with an interesting cupola. It's thought to have been designed by D.M. Craik and is still run by the Portuguese Mission.

St Joseph's Church

# New Bugis Street & Bugis Junction. . . .

With St Joseph's Church on your left, walk down Victoria St until you arrive at a street called New Bugis St, a narrow alley crammed with little stores selling all sorts of merchandise, from watches, bags and clothes, to fresh fruit and local food. Bugis was originally one of the most interesting and louche areas of the city, with hawker stalls by day and bars with transvestites by night. This area was demolished in 1985 to make way for the Bugis MRT station. In 1989 it was proposed that a sanitised version be recreated as a family entertainment area in a new location nearby. The original Bugis St is now under Bugis Junction — an office, hotel and shopping complex. Roofed in glass and air-conditioned, this complex consists of a series of original shophouse façades masking concrete structures.

*Link to the Kampong Gelam walk: Continue down Victoria St in the same direction until you come to Arab St. Turn right onto Arab St and then left down North Bridge Rd.*

# Kampong Gelam

**Nearest MRT: Bugis**
**Approximate walking time: 30 minutes**

## Malay/Muslim Quarter

Kampong Gelam was the home of Malay royalty before the time of
Raffles. It takes its name from the Glam (Eucalyptus) trees which
used to grow here, from which the Bugis and Malays extracted oils
for medicines and to make their ships watertight. Raffles had
allocated this land to Bugis, Arab and other Muslim merchants.
Although the villas on Beach Road have long disappeared, this area
still has a few nice shophouses and residential terraces, as well as
the restored Sultan's palace and the regal Sultan Mosque.

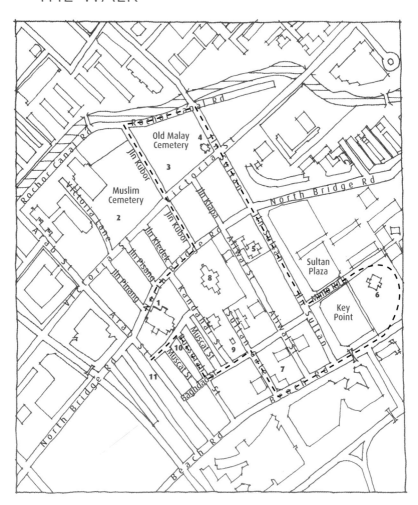

# KEY

1. Sultan Mosque
2. Muslim Cemetery
3. Old Malay Cemetery
4. Malabar Mosque
5. Alsagoff Arab School
6. Hajjah Fatimah Mosque
7. 321 Beach Road
8. Taman Warisan Melayu
9. Kandahar Street
10. Bussorah Mall
11. Arab Street

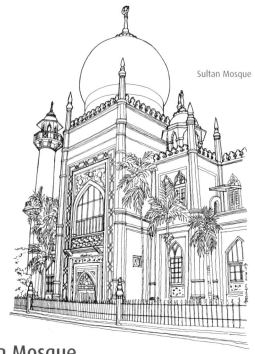

Sultan Mosque

# Sultan Mosque. . . .

**Did You Know?**
The base of this mosque's gilded dome is decorated with bottles.

From Bugis MRT, walk along Victoria St with your back to Bugis Junction, turning right at Ophir Rd. Take the first left down North Bridge Rd. After the Arab St junction, you will see the Sultan Mosque on your right. This is one of Singapore's most spectacular religious buildings and a focal point for Muslims. Thought to be designed by Irish architect Denis Santry of Swan & Maclaren and built in 1924, it was named in honour of the Sultan of Singapore and originally part of his enclave. It's the principal mosque of the 80 or so on the island. It's an attractive mix of Western Classical and Arabic designs, which form a recognisable Muslim style. The first mosque on this site was built in 1824 with a grant of £3,000 from the East India Company. North Bridge Rd was slightly diverted to avoid going through the mosque.

# Muslim Cemetery & Old Malay Cemetery. . . .

Continue down North Bridge Rd and turn left down Jln Kubor. At the junction of Jln Kubor and Victoria St, you will see the Muslim Cemetery on your left and the Old Malay Cemetery opposite it. Dating from about 1819 this is the oldest recorded Malay cemetery in Singapore. J.B. Tassin's map of 1836 labels this area "Tombs of the Malayan Princes". Secluded and quiet, it's romantically overgrown and full of interestingly shaped headstones. Located across Jln Kubor from the Old Malay Cemetery is the Muslim Cemetery which is larger and more open but still quiet, also with the same striking headstones.

# Malabar Mosque. . . .

When you get to the end of Jln Kubor, turn right along Rochor Canal Rd and right again at Jln Sultan. At the junction of Jln Sultan and Victoria St is the Malabar Mosque. This is a small, charming mosque, traditional in its form and layout and best seen in the evening when lit up. Its exterior, however, is clad in a rather unpleasant mix of blue and white tiles. Behind it lies a small, disused cemetery for Malabar Indians. The mosque was built by A.H. Siddique, an immigrant from northern India in the 1920s, who designed a number of buildings in Singapore. It's said he refused to take fees for designing religious buildings.

# Alsagoff Arab School. . . .

Farther down Jln Sultan, on the right after the North Bridge Rd junction is the Alsagoff Arab School. This school is one of the few Islamic religious centres in Singapore. Founded by the Alsagoff family, it has students from Singapore, Malaysia, Brunei and Thailand. Built in 1912, it's a simple two-storeyed design with semicircular arches on pillars and an odd-shaped pediment over the portico. A new wing, in an unsuccessful pastiche, was added in 1992. Jln Sultan's Chinese name is Ji Chap Keng (Twenty Houses), but most of these 20 are no longer standing.

# Hajjah Fatimah Mosque. . . .

**Did You Know?**
This is one of the few mosques on the island named after a woman.

Continuing along Jln Sultan, turn left onto Minto Rd, a small street located between Sultan Plaza and Key Point. Follow Minto Rd to its end and you will see Hajjah Fatimah Mosque on your right. Built in 1846, it is named after its female benefactor, Hajjah Fatimah, a Malaccan lady said to be married to the Sultan of Gowa in the Celebes. This is the oldest

Hajjah Fatimah Mosque

mosque in Singapore. It has been painted brown and cream and has a Malaccan-style neoclassical minaret which leans towards the dome. Altered in 1932 (by the French firm Brossard Mopin who used Malay labour) and repaired in 1973, it is nestled attractively in a large and pleasant open space between the surrounding tall buildings.

321 Beach Rd

# 321 Beach Road. . . .

Walk around the Hajjah Fatimah Mosque and out through the park in front of it onto Beach Rd. Turn right, following Beach Rd until you come to the street called Sultan Gate. At the corner, on the right, is a well-balanced and nicely proportioned three-storeyed art deco building. Its architectural style is strikingly different from that of the rest of the area.

# Taman Warisan Melayu. . . .

At the end of Sultan Gate is Taman Warisan Melayu or Istana Kampong Gelam Heritage Park, which incorporates a Museum of Malay Culture and History, performance areas, souvenir shops and ancillary facilities, including a Malay restaurant. This was the work of the Malay Heritage Foundation and the National Heritage Board, with the Public Works Department (now called CPG Consultants) acting as consultants. It is scheduled to open in December 2004.

Istana Kampong Gelam.

### A. Istana Kampong Gelam

*Istana* means "palace" in Malay. Istana Kampong Gelam is a fine, well-proportioned building. It was built for the last sultan of Singapore between 1836 and 1843 on the site of his original wood and *attap* palace. Because of the style of the porch and the front façade, it's thought to be the work of G.D. Coleman. Sultan Hussein and Temenggong Abdul Rahman ceded Singapore to the East India Company forever in 1824, losing all sovereign rights. An earlier agreement allowed Kampong Gelam to remain in the sultan's family for as long as they lived here. This was repealed in 1897, but the last of his descendants moved out of the premises only in 1999.

### B. Gedung Kuning

№ 73 Sultan Gate is known as Gedung Kuning (Yellow Villa) in Malay and was built in the 1920s for the *bendahara* (the highest official of the *kampong*, a post akin to a treasurer).

# Kandahar Street. . . .

Walk back down Sultan Gate, turn right onto Baghdad St and right again onto Kandahar St. (This street was named after Kandahar, a city in south-central Afghanistan, originally part of the British Empire.) Kandahar St was the site of a *Sook Ching* (mass execution of suspected rebels) during the Japanese Occupation. This street consists of a row of decorative Late Style shophouses, №s 44–54 are especially ornate.

Bussorah Mall

## Bussorah Mall. . . .

Returning to Baghdad St, the second street on your right is Bussorah St, also known as Bussorah Mall. Presumably named after the East India Company factory and residency at Bussorah in the late 18th century, this street and mall was recently restored and pedestrianised. The URA intends this street to be used as a festival street, with hawker stalls and related activities set up here during the Muslim holy month of Ramadan. Bussorah Mall has one of the most striking views of the Sultan Mosque.

## Arab Street. . . .

Back at Baghdad St, with Bussorah Mall behind, turn right and walk until you come to Arab St at the T-junction. Named for Singapore's substantial Arab community who were responsible for bringing trade and the Islamic faith to the region, this is one of the liveliest streets in the city and is famous for its wide variety of handcrafted goods and textiles.

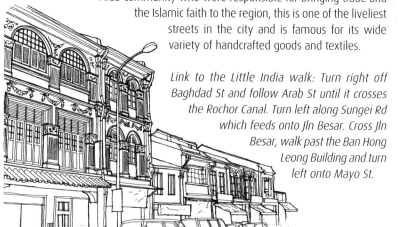

*Link to the Little India walk: Turn right off Baghdad St and follow Arab St until it crosses the Rochor Canal. Turn left along Sungei Rd which feeds onto Jln Besar. Cross Jln Besar, walk past the Ban Hong Leong Building and turn left onto Mayo St.*

Arab Street

# Little India

**Nearest MRT: Bugis**
**Approximate walking time: 50 minutes**

## Indian Quarter

This whole area making up Little India today was a swamp in the late 19th century. The government later set up its own brick kiln and lime pits in the late 1920s. The first recorded brick business on the island was established by an Indian, Naraina Pillai, who came to Singapore with Raffles in 1819. Pillai also founded the Sri Mariamman Temple (in Chinatown) in 1827. Serangoon Road rapidly became the centre of Indian life because of the thriving brick and cattle industries. Although the kilns were closed in 1860, and cattle banned from the area by the government in 1936, Indians continued to live and work here. Today, Little India is still a thriving, bustling place crammed with small shops selling all things Indian, from spices to sarees.

# THE WALK

See detailed map on page 91

# KEY

1. Abdul Gaffoor Mosque
2. Little India Arcade
3. Zhu Jiao Centre
4. Serangoon Road
5. 37 Kerbau Road
6. Sri Lakshminarayan Temple
7. Sri Veeramakaliamman Temple
8. Sri Srinivasa Perumal Temple
9. Leong San See Temple
10. Sakyamuni Buddha Gaya
11. Petain Road
12. Jalan Besar

Little India

Abdul Gaffoor Mosque

# Abdul Gaffoor Mosque. . . .

From Bugis MRT, follow Rochor Rd away from Bugis Junction in the same direction as the traffic. When you reach Rochor Canal, cross the canal onto Jalan Besar, and Mayo St will be the first turn on your left.

Walking down Mayo St, with your back to Jln Besar, you will see the Abdul Gaffoor Mosque on your right. A wooden mosque was built here in 1881 on land leased by Sheikh Abdul Gaffoor bin Shaik Hyder in 1859. He financed its construction by leasing shophouses he had built in the 1880s. It was replaced by the present mosque in 1907. Although similar to other mosques, this is unusually symmetrical in layout and has more classical detailing. The dome and minarets are finely modelled. There's a pleasant space between the front of the mosque and the row of shophouses (c.1918) opposite. Many Indian Muslims worship at this mosque.

# Little India Arcade. . . .

Continue to the end of Mayo St, turn right onto Perak Rd, left at Dunlop St and left again onto Clive St. Between Campbell Lane and Hastings Rd, on your right, you will see Little India Arcade. This is a block of renovated shophouses containing souvenir shops. The attempt to retain the original character of the area is more successful here than in similar attempts made in Chinatown.

# Zhu Jiao Centre. . . .

Exit the Little India Arcade via the Serangoon Rd exit, and you will see the Zhu Jiao Centre on the opposite side of Serangoon Rd. This is a lively wholesale and retail fresh produce market, with numerous food stalls selling Indian food in the hawker centre located upstairs. Built by the Housing Development Board (HDB) in 1981, it replaced the Kandang Kerbau Market, a fine building which was knocked down when Bukit Timah Rd was widened. The new building is reasonably well-designed (it won the Singapore Institute of Architects' Outstanding Building Prize in 1983) but slightly out of scale with its neighbours.

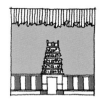

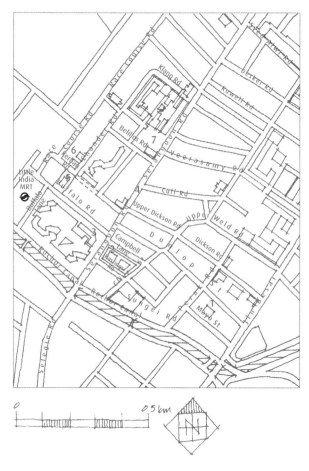

## Key

1. Abdul Gaffoor Mosque
2. Little India Arcade
3. Zhu Jiao Centre
4. Serangoon Road
5. 37 Kerbau Road
6. Sri Lakshminarayan Temple
7. Sri Veeramakaliamman Temple

Little India

## Serangoon Road. . . .

One of the earliest roads to be built in Singapore, Serangoon Rd might have been named after storks (*burung ranggong* being Malay for stork) which used to inhabit the swampland here. It was labelled "proposed road across the island" on an 1822 map reconstructed by C.A. Gibson-Hill. The streets in the area were originally lanes leading to the private residences of Europeans. The majority of Indians that settled here were Chettiars, a caste of money-lenders from South India. There are some fine examples of First Transitional Style shophouses here.

## 37 Kerbau Road. . . .

**Did You Know?**
Kerbau Rd got its name from the Malay word for buffalo because cattle used to be kept near the abattoirs here.

Follow Buffalo Rd along the side of Zhu Jiao Centre all the way to the end, turn right onto Race Course Rd, which veers to the right, then keep going as it turns onto Kerbau Rd and you will see № 37 on your right. Tan Tang Niah's eight-room house was built here in 1900 and restored by the HDB in 1990. On either side of the entrance portico, there are carriage gates leading into courtyards. Over the entrance is a gilded nameplate with the calligraphic inscription *Siew Song* (Refined Pine); the pine being a symbol of endurance to the Chinese.

37 Kerbau Rd

## Sri Lakshminarayan Temple. . . .

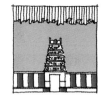

Continue walking down Kerbau Rd a little until you see Chander Rd on your left. The Sri Lakshminarayan Temple will be one of the first temples you will see on the left side of Chander Rd. This North Indian Hindu temple is dedicated to Lakshmi, an incarnation of the goddess Kali. Its red, pointed domes are prominent features in the neighbourhood and lend interest to an otherwise unremarkable building.

## Sri Veeramakaliamman Temple. . . .

Follow Chander Rd as far as Belilios Rd. Walk to the end of Belilios Rd, where it meets Serangoon Rd, and you will see Sri Veeramakliamman Temple on the left. Built in the early 1880s by the Bengali community and dedicated to the Indian goddess Kali, this temple has a standard layout with a worship hall and a *gopuram* that features the usual range of polychromatic gods. Kali, the Sanskrit word for black, is a devouring Hindu goddess. Daily goat sacrifices are a common offering to her.

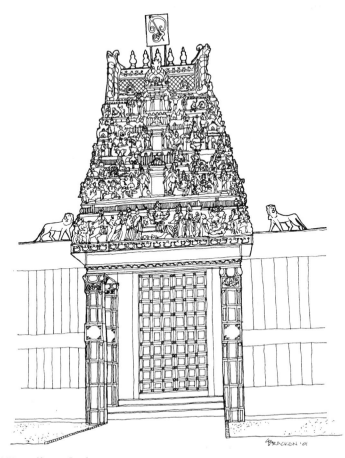

Sri Veeramakliamman Temple

# Sri Srinivasa Perumal Temple. . . .

From Belilios Rd, turn left onto Serangoon Rd and walk to the Sri Srinivasa Perumal Temple, about eight blocks away, on the left side of the road. It's not known exactly when this temple was built, but a Mr Narasinghan bought the site from the East India Company in 1855. It was almost completely rebuilt between 1961 and 1966, when South Indian sculptors executed the motifs on the roof and a marriage hall was erected. The seemingly older *gopuram* (representing the five manifestations of Vishnu) was only added in 1979. It's also the starting point for the annual Thaipusam festival procession which ends at the Sri Dhandayuthapani (Chettiar) Temple on Tank Rd.

Note: Thaipusam

This is a Hindu festival of penance or thanks for a wish granted, preceded by a period of prayer and diet restrictions believed to purify the soul. Devotees walk barefoot along a 3-kilometre (1.9-mile) route, carrying a heavy steel framework (or *kavadi*) weighing about 32 kilogrammes (70.5 pounds). This structure is adorned with limes, images of gods, small vessels of milk, and peacock feathers and secured to the flesh with small hooks. Devotees' cheeks and tongues are pierced with skewers, and the word *vel* chanted along the route, in memory of the *vell* (lance) of Lord Shiva, which was used to deflect demons. Women's cheeks and tongues are also pierced, but they carry only a half-*kavadi*.

# Leong San See Temple. . . .

Continue down Serangoon Rd and take the first left down the laneway opposite Beatty Rd. At the top of this laneway, after crossing Race Course Rd at the T-junction, you will see the Leong San See Temple. Also known as Dragon Mountain Temple, it was founded in 1917 by Chan Lin, a Buddhist monk. It was later expanded by Tan Boo Liat, a local merchant. Dedicated to Guan Yin, the Goddess of Mercy, its main hall accommodates both Guan Yin and the Sakyamuni Buddha. A fine temple in a Chinese palace style, it has been marred by some insensitive additions. Look out also for the majestic stone lions at the entrance and the elaborate ceramic carvings of dragons, phoenixes and flowers on the roof.

# Sakyamuni Buddha Gaya. . . .

Slightly farther down Race Course Rd, with the Leong San See Temple on your right, is the Sakyamuni Buddha Gaya on your left. It is also known as the Temple of the Thousand Lights because of the number of coloured lights illuminating the 15-metre (49-foot) statue of Buddha. It is possible to walk inside the statue, where you will see another smaller one. Built in 1927 by a Thai monk called Vutthisasara, it's reminiscent of a Thai *wat* (temple), and shows both Chinese and Indian cultural influences.

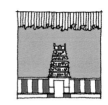

Sakyamuni Buddha Gaya

Petain Rd

## Petain Road. . . .

Return to the laneway, turn right onto Serangoon Rd and take the second left onto Petain Rd, which contains a terrace of shophouses, one of the best preserved in Singapore. They were built in the 1930s by J.M. Jackson and feature ceramic wall tiles in many pastel colours from France, Belgium and Japan. These tiles are painted with motifs such as flowers, birds and mythological Chinese creatures.

## Jalan Besar. . . .

Continue down Petain Rd, turning right at Jln Besar. Laid out in the 1880s, Jln Besar ("big road" in Malay) contains shophouses that range in style from the First Transitional to Art Deco. Many of them are also painted pastel shades. (In the Malay and Peranakan cultures, pink is a sign of good fortune and happiness, while green represents spring, permanency and peace.) Follow Jln Besar to its junction with Sungei Rd at Rochor Canal.

*Link to the Orchard Rd walk: Follow Sungei Rd toward Rochor Canal, and turn left onto Selegie Rd.*

Jalan Besar

# Orchard Road

**Nearest MRT: Dhoby Ghaut**
**Approximate walking time: 40 minutes**

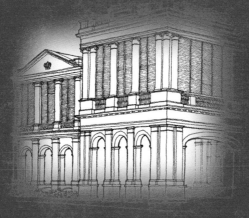

## Peranakan Quarter

Orchard Road was so named because of the numerous nutmeg and pepper plantations which originally lined it. Back then, it was a pleasant, narrow, tree-lined road crossed by a railway line until the 1930s. Many of the roads surrounding Orchard Rd were named after former estate owners: Prinsep, Oxley, Cairnhill and Cuppage. The first shophouses were built here in the 1880s. It is said that a tiger was spotted along Orchard Road even as late as 1948. Today, Orchard Rd is one of Asia's premier shopping streets and a favourite haunt for many Singaporeans on weekends.

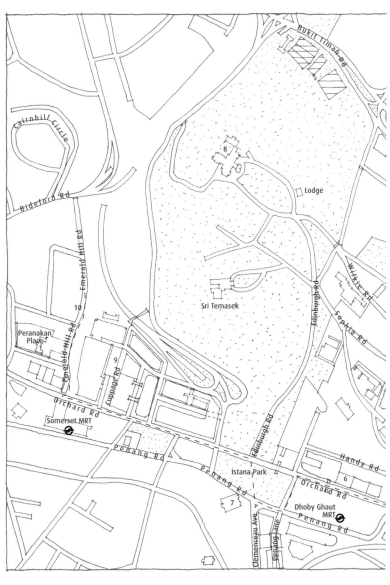

## Key

1. Ellison Building
2. Niven Road
3. David Elias Building
4. Cathay Building
5. Orchard Presbyterian Church
6. MacDonald House
7. Tan Yeok Nee House
8. Istana
9. Cuppage Terrace
10. Emerald Hill Road

Orchard Road

Ellison Building

# Ellison Building. . . .

When you emerge from Dhoby Ghaut MRT Station, walk in the direction of Selegie Rd, following the road until you apprpach Rochor Canal Rd. You will see the Ellison Building taking up the last block on your left at the corner of Selegie and MacKenzie Rds. A pleasant two-storeyed corner building from 1924, it's nicely detailed with curved balconies, Doric columns and pilasters, as well as a cupola at either end of the Selegie Rd façade. The Star of David is prominent at the cornice level and reflects the building's original owners.

> **Did You Know?**
> Selegie Rd originally consisted of convict-built shophouses, few of which have survived among the modern shopping complexes. Selegie Rd was possibly named after *bukit selegi*, a native wooden spear sharpened and hardened by fire, or the *orang selegi*, a Bugis pirate race that settled in Singapore in Raffles' time.

# Niven Road. . . .

Walk along MacKenzie Rd, and turn left onto Niven Rd. This road, named after Lawrence Niven, a superintendent of the Botanic Gardens, consists of simple but pleasant two-storeyed terraces, complete with *pintu pagars* (saloon

doors) and rusticated columns and jalousies (adjustable slatted shutters). At the corner of Niven Rd and Wilkie Rd, on your right, stands Wilkie House, a good, but run-down, art deco building.

CKEN AUG '03

## David Elias Building. . . .

Follow Niven Rd to the end and turn left onto Wilkie Rd. Overlooking the junction of Selegie Rd and Middle Rd is the David Elias Building. This three-storeyed block of shops and offices, done in a stripped down neoclassical style by Swan & Maclaren in 1928, dominates this important junction and lends definition and dignity to the streetscape. The balconies and projecting concrete slab, at eaves level, gives it a slightly art deco look. As with the Ellison Building, the Star of David is a prominent decorative feature.

## Cathay Building. . . .

Turning right from Wilkie Rd onto Selegie Rd, walk down it until it becomes Prinsep St. At the end of Prinsep St, turn right onto Bras Basah Rd. You will come soon to what is left of the Cathay Building (or Cathay Cinema) on your right, sandwiched in between Kirk Terrace and Handy Rd. This 1939 building by Frank Brewer was the first skyscraper in the city. Its clever circulation used the awkward topography of the site but, unfortunately, the ugly cladding added in 1978 obliterated his original design. It was home to the British Malaya Broadcasting Corporation until the Japanese Occupation, when it was used as the headquarters for the Japanese propaganda department. It was, in turn, used by Lord Mountbatten as the headquarters for the Japanese surrender in 1945. The building in under construction, and the façade has been retained.

**Did You Know?**
Bras Basah Rd used to be lined with secondhand bookshops specialising in school textbooks. Lee Kuan Yew was walking here in early 1942, shortly after Singapore fell to the Japanese, when he noticed a crowd gathered in front of the Cathay Building. Joining the crowd, he saw the head of a Chinese man on a pole with a notice in Chinese (which he could not read at the time) saying that this was what happened to people who broke the law (the man had been caught looting). He immediately visited one of the neighbouring bookshops and bought himself a book on how to learn Chinese (Chiang Ker Chiu's *Mandarin Made Easy*) to ensure that he would be able to read such notices in the future. This event also impressed upon Lee the fact that strict punishment reduced crime, something he would later introduce into his administration.

Orchard Road

MacDonald House

# Orchard Presbyterian Church. . . .

Bras Basah Rd merges with Orchard Rd at this point. Across this road is the Orchard Presbyterian Church. The site on which it stands was granted by the governor of Singapore in 1875 for the building of a church. Nicely proportioned with well-executed Palladian detailing, it was completed in 1878. In 1975, it was enlarged and modernised. A further extension was carried out in the 1980s.

# MacDonald House. . . .

With your back to the Orchard Presbyterian Church and with Cathay Building on your right, walk down Orchard Rd and you will see MacDonald House on the right. This well-proportioned red brick building was one of Palmer & Turner's first commissions in Singapore. Built in 1949 for the Hong Kong and Shanghai Banking Corporation, it was the scene of a fatal bombing on 10 March 1965, when three people were killed and 33 injured. At that time, Indonesia strongly objected to Singapore being part of the newly independent Malaysia and ran a terrorist bombing campaign known as the Konfrontasi.

# Tan Yeok Nee House. . . .

Take the first left onto Penang Lane, keeping the Istana Park on your right. Turn right onto Penang Rd, and you will see Tan Yeok Nee House across the road from the park. Built around 1885 using granite columns and carvings from China, this free-standing townhouse, built for a wealthy Teochew gambier and pepper merchant, was home to many occupants: the station-master for the railway line that ran across Orchard Rd, a bishop and boarders from St Mary's House and School for Girls. The building was also used by the Japanese army during their occupation and later, by the Salvation Army.

This building style was popular in southern China at the time the Tan Yeok Nee House was built but is now unique in Singapore (the other three houses built in this style have since been demolished). Restored in 2000, it is now the University of Chicago Graduate Business School.

Tan Yeok Nee House

BRACKEN '01

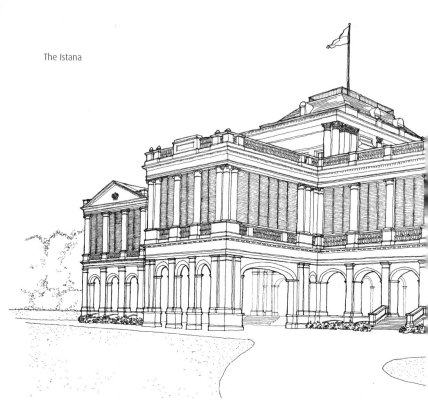

The Istana

# Istana. . . .

Cutting through Istana Park and crossing Orchard Rd, you will see the Istana gates in front of you. Before being bought by Governor Sir Harry Ord for Government House, the Istana demesne was a large nutmeg plantation belonging to Charles Prinsep.

The building itself, designed by J.F.A. McNair, was built in 1869 by Indian convict labour. It's a not badly proportioned two-storeyed neoclassical white block which rises to a third storey with a squat, centrally placed tower. The demesne also includes Sri Temasek (c.1869) — a wooden building with deep verandahs in the style of the Malay house. Originally built for the colonial secretary, the Istana is now the official residence of Singapore's president. Other buildings consist of the Annexe, the Istana Villa (c.1938) and the Lodge (c.1974). The grounds are beautifully maintained, containing a 9-hole golf course and a terrace garden. It's only open to the public on national holidays, but it is well worth a visit. It's best to go early as it can get very crowded.

**Istana**
http://www.istana.gov.sg/openhouse.htnl
Opened on some public holidays from 8am to 6.30 pm.
Dates are published on the website or in the local newspapers
Admission: Free for Singaporeans and Singaporean Permanent Residents. Others, including foreign visitors, are required to pay an entrance fee of S$1 per person.

# Cuppage Terrace. . . .

With your back to the Istana entrance, turn right along Orchard Rd until you get to Cuppage Rd (about the fifth turning on your right). At the end of Cuppage Rd is Cuppage Terrace, which overlooks a pedestrianised plaza. This is a renovated terrace of fine Malaccan-Peranakan style shophouses dating from the 1920s, now mostly home to bars and restaurants.

Cuppage Terrace is named after William Cuppage who worked his way up though the colonial postal service and owned a nutmeg estate here until the 1860s. His son-in-law, Edwin Koek, sold the land and was declared bankrupt in 1891. Cuppage's home, Fern Cottage, built in the 1850s, was the first Dutch Club before being knocked down by the new Chinese owners in 1906 to make way for the development of shophouses.

**Note: Peranakan Culture**

Chinese traders visited Malacca from the earliest days of its settlement. By the 15th century, Malacca had become one of the most important ports for Chinese trade missions. Some of these Chinese traders intermarried with the local Malays and settled around Bukit Cina (Chinese Hill). Subsequent generations were called Straits Chinese or Peranakan (which means "born here" in Malay.) The women were called Nyonyas and the men, Babas. They created a sophisticated and influential society, and became known for their shrewd business acumen and opulent lifestyles. The Nyonyas adopted Malay dress and were renowned for the intricate jewellery and beadwork slippers.

The Golden Age of the Peranakans was in the 18th and 19th centuries. Their upper classes assimilated easily into British colonial society from the late 1820s, embracing Western ideas and evolving their own Malay dialect. The turn of the 20th century also saw a gradual substitution of the Baba's language by the Hokkien dialect and the conversion of many Peranakans from Buddhism to Christianity. One of their most enduring legacies is their spicy cuisine, the result of the blending of Chinese and local Malayan Peninsula ingredients, most notably *belacan* (prawn paste) and coconut milk.

# Emerald Hill Road. . . .

Walking back down Cuppage Rd onto Orchard Rd, turn right and follow Orchard Rd until you come to the pedestrianised entrance to Emerald Hill Rd. Follow it as it winds its way up a gentle slope. This area was primeval jungle when Raffles landed. Between 1819 and 1836, the jungles were cleared to provide fuel for the boiling of gambier leaves. Then part of the nutmeg plantation belonging to William Cuppage, this area was subdivided in the early 20th century for the building of shophouses. The first houses were built by Teochews and Peranakans. Hokkiens also moved here from Amoy and Telok Ayer Sts in Chinatown. The 2- to 3-storeyed houses here are of differing designs and are richly detailed.

*Link to the Botanic Gardens walk: Walk to the end of Emerald Hill Rd and turn left onto Cairnhill Circle. Take the second right onto Cairnhill Rd. At the end, turn left onto Scotts Rd.*

Emerald Hill Rd

# Botanic Gardens

**Nearest MRT: Newton**
**Approximate walking time: 45 minutes**

## Colonial Quarter

Always an up-market enclave, the Nassim Road area is now home to many embassies, hotels and some fine black-and-white colonial bungalows. The Chinese called Tanglin Road *Tua Tangleng* (meaning "great east hill peaks") in the 1840s, as there were several hills in the area. The Teochews were unhappy with Raffles' allotment of land in 1822 and ventured into Tanglin, then tiger-infested country, where they grew pepper, nutmeg and gambier. The Europeans, many of them Scottish, later opened plantations and built villas here, leaving behind place names such as Balmoral, Claymore and Tyersall.

# THE WALK

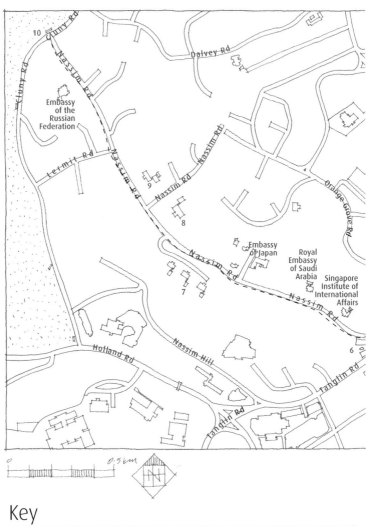

## Key

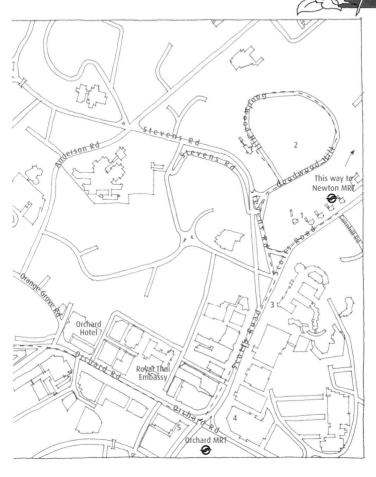

6. Nassim Jade Condominium

7. 23–27 Nassim Road

8. Eden Hall (28 Nassim Road)

9. Boscombe (40 Nassim Road)

10. Singapore Botanic Gardens

Botanic Gardens

35A Scotts Rd

## Scotts Road. . . .

If you are coming from Newton MRT, walk along Scotts Rd in the direction of the city, passing Cairnhill Rd on your left. You can still see some fine bungalows on the right of the road. This area used to be plantation land. Grand mansions were built here in the early 20th century.

This road was named after Captain William Scott — first cousin of the writer Sir Walter Scott, son of James Scott, who was a pioneer settler of Penang and advisor to Sir Francis Light, founder of Georgetown. Harbour Master and Post Master of Singapore in 1836, Captain Scott also owned a large plantation in Claymore, which grew betel-nut, rambutan, chiku, mangosteen, durian, sea cotton, arrowroot, and cocoa.

## Goodwood Hill. . . .

Turn right up Stevens Rd and right again up Goodwood Hill. Well-planted with large, mature trees, this area has one of the largest intact collections of 1920s black-and-white colonial bungalows on the island, quite a number of which can be seen from the road.

## Goodwood Park Hotel. . . .

Goodwood Hill forms a circle, taking you back out onto Stevens Rd. Walk down Stevens Rd until it merges with Scotts Rd, and you will see Goodwood Park Hotel on your left. Its tower wing is a national monument and was designed by R.A.J. Bidwell of Swan & Maclaren in 1900. Despite its imposing site and its dramatic Victorian profile, it seems less impressive than the more

restrained Raffles Hotel, which Bidwell completed in 1899. Originally called the Teutonia Club, it was intended for the German residents of Singapore but was confiscated by the colonial authorities at the outbreak of World War I. When the Manasseh Brothers bought it in 1918, they renamed it Goodwood Hall. Converted to a hotel in 1929, it was occupied by the Australian Army at the end of World War II for the investigation of Japanese war crimes. It has been unsympathetically extended.

## Marriott Hotel. . . .

Continue along Scotts Rd to the Orchard Rd junction. The Marriott Hotel occupies this corner. Originally built in 1982 as the Dynasty Hotel, this 33-storeyed octagonal tower, capped by a pagoda-style Chinese roof, is one of the few modern buildings in Singapore to incorporate Chinese architectural features. The hotel's open-air bar is a pleasant place to sit and watch the bustling junction.

Goodwood Park Hotel

## Wheelock Place. . . .

Diagonally opposite Marriott Hotel, at the corner of Orchard and Paterson Roads, is Wheelock Place, home to Borders bookshop. Designed in 1994 by Japanese architect Kisho Kurokawa, its distinctive glass cone elegantly marks the entrance to this seven-storeyed shopping complex, which also incorporates a 16-storeyed office tower overlooking Orchard Boulevard at its rear.

## Nassim Road. . . .

Walk along Orchard Rd with Wheelock Place on your left. After passing Orchard Hotel on your left, instead of continuing left down Tanglin Rd, take a right down Nassim Rd. This road is home to some embassies, a number of modern but generally badly proportioned villas and some fine black-and-white colonial bungalows (notably Nºs 6, 8, 23, 25 and 27), all of which can be seen easily from the road.

> **Did You Know?**
> Nassim Rd was named after a prominent Jewish family whose house was called Nassim Lodge. The Nassims later sold property on Orchard Rd to C.K. Tang. Some of the Nassim family have since moved to Israel.

# Nassim Jade Condominium. . . .

At the beginning of Nassim Rd, on the left, is the Nassim Jade Condominium. The earlier building on this site, the Jade House, was built in 1926 by Chung & Wong Architects and was the private villa of Aw Boon Haw, owner of the Tiger Balm Company. It was thought that an American architect was also involved in the building of this house, in an attempt to make it resemble the White House in Washington D.C. (which it didn't). Aw Boon Haw's famous jade collection was exhibited here (the portion of the house housing his jade collection was open to the public until 1979). The collection was then transferred to the Singapore History Museum.

The old building was demolished by the Urban Redevelopment Authority (URA) in 1990. On this site now stands the Nassim Jade Condominium, built in 1997 by Chan Sau Yan Architects. They, thankfully, didn't try to make any architectural references to the Jade House, which was a rather ugly building. Instead, they designed an attractive contemporary apartment complex with clean lines and materials appropriate for its environment, such as attractive wooden shutters along the front façade.

Nassim Jade Condominium

# Eden Hall. . . .

Farther down Nassim Rd, on the right side, is Eden Hall at № 28. This is the residence of the British High Commissioner. A large Victorian bungalow, its grounds are open to the public once a year during the Eden Hall Fair, usually celebrated in October. Designed by Swan & Maclaren, its symmetrical façade is highly decorated with simulated stonework and plaster relief.

The land on which Eden Hall stands was bought by Saul Jacob Nathan, a partner of S. Manasseh & Company in 1903. The senior partner of the firm, Ezekial Saleh Manasseh, built the house in 1904, residing there from 1918 until his death in 1945. Between 1904 and 1918, the house was used as a boarding house. The cast-iron balustrades of the main staircase still carry the monogram "M", probably at the request of Manasseh or his architects.

# Boscombe. . . .

At № 40, also located on the right, is a large, rather plain, white, neoclassical bungalow. It was the former residence of the U.S. Naval Attache to Singapore.

# Singapore Botanic Gardens. . . .

Continue along Nassim Rd. Turn right at the Cluny Rd junction, and you will see the entrance to the Singapore Botanic Gardens. The first Botanic Gardens was founded by Raffles in 1822 on Singapore Hill (now Fort Canning Park) and called the Botanical and Experimental Garden or Spice Garden. (See the *Fort Canning Park* chapter for more on the Spice Garden.) The present gardens were founded in 1859 but not opened to the public until 1874 when the government took over and established a zoo there (which lasted until 1905). Lawrence Niven, a nutmeg planter, supervised the layout of the 32-hectare gardens between 1859 and 1875.

National Parks Headquarters, Singapore Botanic Gardens

E.J.H. Corner House

The gardens contain four hectares of rainforest, thousands of species of trees, an orchid garden, the visitor centre, Burkill Hall (a black-and-white colonial bungalow built in 1866 and formerly home to the garden directors), the Gardens Office (dated 1882) and E.J.H. Corner House (another black-and-white colonial bungalow now home to the up-market French restaurant, Les Amis). The national flower, the Vanda Miss Joaquim orchid, also blooms here.

**Did You Know?**
The first rubber seedlings came to the Botanic Gardens from Kew Gardens in London in 1877. But it was only when Henry Ridley became the garden's director in 1888 that the trees, originally from Brazil, started to thrive. Known as "Mad" Ridley for his efforts to persuade Malayan coffee planters to grow rubber, he single-handedly founded the Malayan rubber industry in 1897, succeeding in tapping rubber without damaging the tree's bark.

### Singapore Botanic Gardens
Visitor Service Desk
1 Cluny Rd. Tel: 6471 7361
http://www.sbg.org.sg
Open daily from 5am to midnight
Admission to Gardens: Free
Admission to National Orchid Garden: Adults S$2,
students (under 12) and senior citizens (over 60) S$1

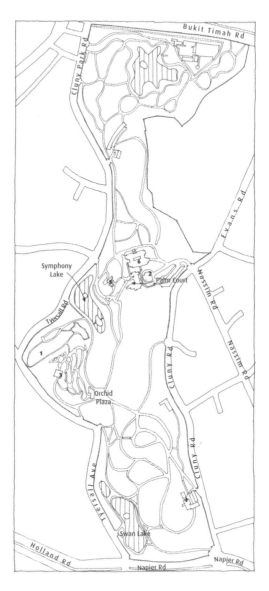

## Key: Singapore Botanic Gardens

1. National Orchid Garden
2. Visitors' Centre
3. Burkill Hall
4. Gardens Office
5. E.J.H Corner House
6. National Parks Headquarters

# Further Afield

## Further Afield

This chapter covers individual, but isolated, architectural gems, such as the Sun Yat Sen Nanyang Memorial Hall. It also covers three outlying areas, not often visited, but with considerable charm and character: the bustling Peranakan enclave along Mountbatten and East Coast Roads; the stately grandeur of colonial life at Telok Blangah and Alexandra Park; and the rustic idyll of Pulau Ubin — a step back in time to the Singapore of an earlier era.

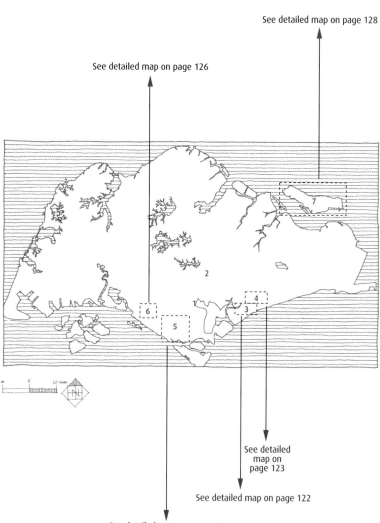

See detailed map on page 128

See detailed map on page 126

See detailed
map on
page 123

See detailed map on page 122

See detailed map on page 125

## KEY

1. Chesed-El Synagogue
2. Sun Yat Sen Nanyang Memorial Hall
3. Mountbatten Road
4. East Coast Road
5. Telok Blangah
6. Alexandra Park
7. Pulau Ubin

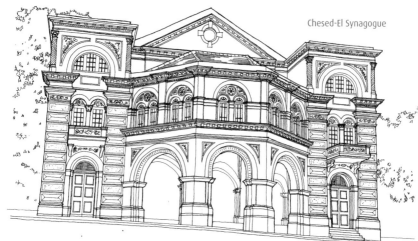

Chesed-El Synagogue

# Chesed-El Synagogue. . . .

Located at № 2 Oxley Rise, the Chesed-El Synagogue can be viewed from the road but is not open to the public. The nearest MRT is Dhoby Ghaut. Exit the MRT station and turn right onto Penang Rd. Take the second left at Clemenceau Ave, following this road until you come to a flyover. Cross under the flyover and take the first right turn up the steep Oxley Rise. You will see the synagogue just before the second turning to the left.

This is one of two Jewish synagogues in the city, the other being the Maghain Aboth on Waterloo St. Simple in form, with finely considered decoration, it was designed in 1905 by R.A.J. Bidwell of Swan & Maclaren and founded by Sir Reuben Manasseh Meyer. Meyer had it built close to his home, Belle Vue (Killiney House), which was demolished in 1982.

# Sun Yat Sen Nanyang Memorial Hall. . . .

This was Dr Sun Yat Sen's residence in Singapore before the overthrow of the Qing Dynasty in China in 1911. Sun's time in Singapore was spent organising secret societies and raising funds for the revolution. The land on which the building stands was once a sugar plantation owned by Joseph Balestier, who was appointed first United States Counsel to Singapore in 1837. The house

Sun Yat Sen Nanyang Memorial Hall

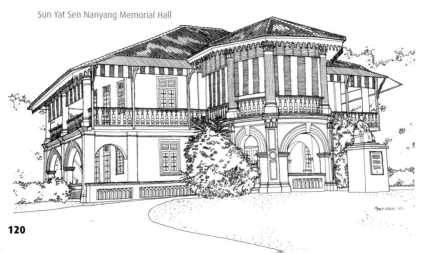

was probably built in the 1880s by Boey Chuan Poh for his concubine. Later, rubber magnate Teo Eng Hock bought the villa for his aged mother. A fervent supporter of the Chinese revolutionary cause, Teo offered the place to Dr Sun for his revolutionary activities in 1906. It was bought by a group of local philanthropists in 1938 and presented to the Singapore Chinese Chamber of Commerce and Industry (SCCCI), who renamed it Sun Yat Sen Nanyang Memorial Hall. An attractive Victorian villa, it's symmetrical and well-scaled, with verandahs and modified Doric and Corinthian pilasters. It was renovated in the mid-1960s and was restored in 2001.

### Sun Yat Sen Nanyang Memorial Hall

12 Tai Gin Rd (off Ah Hood Rd along Balestier Rd). Tel: 6256 7377
http://www.wanqingyuan.com.sg/english
Open from 10am to 5 pm Tues–Sun. Opens until 10pm on Sat.
Admission: Adult S$3, students and senior citizens S$2.
Nearest MRT: Toa Payoh. Then take SBS Transit bus Nºs: 21, 130, 131, 139, 145 or 186 to Balestier Rd. If you take bus Nºs 139 or 145, alight at the third bus stop after the Toa Payoh Interchange. Alternatively, take Nºs 21 or 131 from Thomson Rd (opposite the Novena MRT station) and alight at Balestier Rd (opposite the Moulmein Community Centre).

# Katong & Geylang Serai. . . .

This mini-walk is about 4.5 kilometres (2.8 miles) long and takes you through an enclave of excellent and relatively intact Peranakan architecture. SBS Transit buses 12 & 14 go to Mountbatten Rd and East Coast Rd.

> **Did You Know?**
> Much of Katong & Geylang Serai was once coconut plantation, owned by the Alsagoff family and later sold to Chew Joo Chiat after World War I. This area became built-up in the 1920s and '30s.

Our walk starts with some interesting houses on Mountbatten Rd and the sideroads off it. At Nº 745 Mountbatten Rd stands the art deco Chan's Villa (c.1938), and at Nº 759 is the Victorian-era Sing Hoe Hotel. With these houses on your left, walk along Mountbatten Rd until you can turn right onto Tanjong Katong Rd. Take the second left onto Amber Rd. At Nº 21, you will find the Chinese Swimming Club's rambling buildings, with their distinctive purple-tiled roofs straddling both sides of Amber Rd. A little farther along Amber Rd from the swimming club is an unusually shaped seaside bungalow at Nº 23. This was designed by R.A.J. Bidwell but has been all but ruined by insensitive alterations and has now fallen into disrepair. These two buildings used to be on the seashore before land reclamation in the 1960s. Follow Amber Rd as it veers left. Turn right onto Mountbatten Rd which, at this point, merges with East Coast Rd.

Turn left off East Coast Rd and onto Joo Chiat Rd. Walk along this road for about 500 metres (0.3 miles) until you can turn right onto Koon Seng Rd.

The terraces at the junction of Koon Seng and Joo Chiat Roads are particularly fine. (Should you wish to explore further, there are also well-preserved terraces at Everitt and Onan Roads nearby.)

Continue along Koon Seng Rd until you can turn right onto Still Rd. About 750 metres (0.5 miles) down this road, after St Patrick's Rd on the left, you will see the dilapidated Grand Hotel at 25 Still Rd.

Junction of Koon Seng Rd & Joo Chiat Rd.

Opposite this hotel is a rundown Victorian bungalow at № 26, overlooking the junction of Still Rd with Marine Parade Rd. From here you can see the deconstructivist Marine Parade Community Centre, designed by Singaporean architect William Lim. Turn right before this junction onto the narrow Marine Parade Rd Park, take the fourth right onto Sea Ave and you can't miss the elaborate Victorian bungalow at № 31, its tower overlooking the park. Farther along Sea Avenue, on your right, is another elaborate bungalow at № 25. At the end of Sea Avenue, turn left onto East Coast Rd.

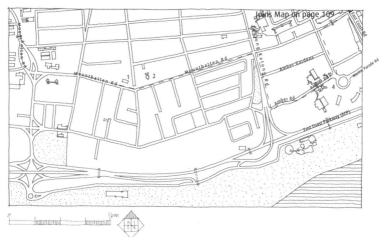

Joins Map on page 109

## Key: Mountbatten Rd

1. Chan's Villa (745 Mountbatten Road)
2. Sing Hoe Hotel (759 Mountbatten Road)
3. Chinese Swimming Club (21 Amber Road)
4. 23 Amber Road

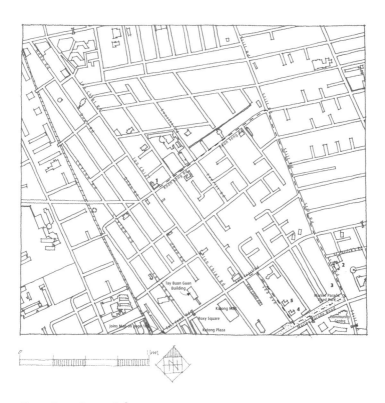

Joins Map on page 109

## Key: East Coast Rd

1. Junction of Koon Seng & Joo Chiat Roads
2. Grand Hotel (25 Still Road)
3. 26 Still Road
4. 31 Sea Ave
5. 25 Sea Ave

Further Afield

# Telok Blangah. . . .

The Telok Blangah walk starts at Mt Faber Rd, where Lower Delta and Kampong Bahru Rds meet. SBS Transit buses 97 & 143 go to Telok Blangah Rd, Kampong Bahru Rd and Lower Delta Rd. Walk up the winding Mt Faber Rd for about 1.25 kilometres (0.8 miles), and you will come to the cable car station on your left. Farther down, you will come to Mt Faber Loop. Take the shorter left fork, which will bring you downhill. At its intersection with Pender Rd, stands the Danish Seaman's Church. The distance is 900 metres (0.6 miles) from the Cable Car Station to the Danish Seaman's Church. The views are spectacular.

## A. Danish Seaman's Church

> **Did You Know?**
> Anna Leonowens (Anna from *The King and I*) is supposed to have been a guest at this house.

This house was built around 1909 by Tan Boon Liat, grandson of important Hokkien pioneer Tan Tock Seng. He was a friend of Dr Sun Yat Sen, who stayed here (illegally) at his invitation in 1911. The house was called Golden Bell then. Sun was en route to Shanghai where he was to become provisional president of the new Republic of China.

3 Canterbury Rd

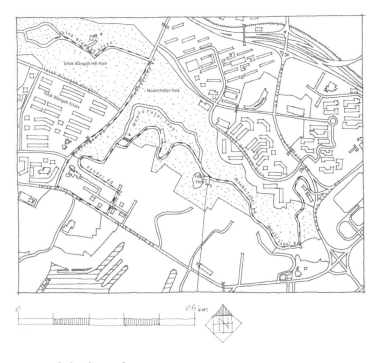

## Key: Telok Blangah

1. Mount Faber (cable car station)
2. Danish Seaman's Church
3. Alkaff Mansion

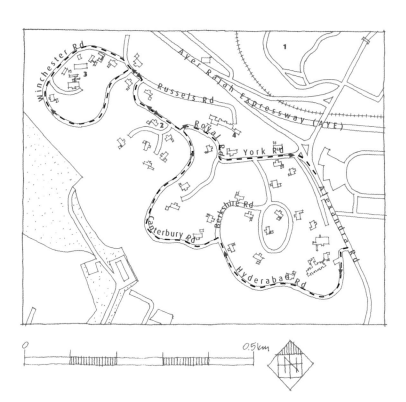

## Key: Alexandra Park

1. Alexandra Hospital
2. 3 Canterbury Road
3. Winchester School (Former)
4. Eton Hall

Winchester School (Former)

## B. Alkaff Mansion

Continue down Pender Rd, turn right onto Morse Rd and right again onto Telok Blangah Rd. Take a right onto Henderson Rd and walk for about 1 kilometre (0.6 miles), passing Telok Blangah residential estate and Telok Blangah Heights on the left. Alternatively, you can take SBS Transit buses 131 or 145 up Henderson Rd for two stops. Turn left onto Telok Blangah Green and walk along this road for about 450 metres (0.3 miles) onto Telok Blangah Hill Park until you come to Alkaff Mansion on the right.

This was used as a weekend hilltop retreat by the wealthy Alkaff family in the 1920s, and has been converted into an up-market Indonesian restaurant. Originally called Mount Washington, it was a venue for decadent parties for both local and international businesspeople, celebrities and dignitaries. A simple symmetrical building perched imposingly at the top of a steep hill approached by a long flight of steps, it commands excellent views of the sea to the south.

### Alkaff Mansion Restaurant

10 Telok Blangah Green. Tel: 6415 4888

## C. Alexandra Park

This is a walk of about 3 kilometres (1.9 miles) in one of the finest colonial residential estates in Singapore. Largely built between 1935 and 1940 by Far East Land to accommodate navy and military personnel, Alexandra Park is located just off Alexandra Rd. (SBS Transit Bus Nºs 97 & 166 run along Alexandra Rd.) More houses were later added here for doctors and technicians from the nearby Alexandra Hospital.

The entire estate has been laid out in the English garden suburb style with each house sitting in a hectare or so of garden. The best way around the Alexandra Park estate is to walk up Hyderabad Rd for about 700 metres (0.4 miles) from Alexandra Rd. At the fork, turn left onto Canterbury Rd. This road is about 900 metres (0.6 miles) long. Nº 3 Canterbury Rd is a typical example of the English garden suburb style. Well-kept and pretty, it is set comfortably back from the road. When Canterbury Rd merges with

Further Afield

Russels Rd, turn left and left again onto Winchester Rd, which is a ring road of about 800 metres (0.5 miles). You will pass the former Winchester School, now a kindergarten. This was built in 1936 as an officers' mess. When you have completed the Winchester Rd walk, rejoin Canterbury Rd via Russels Rd. Take a left onto Royal Rd and a left again onto York Rd, which will lead you back out to Alexandra Rd.

# Pulau Ubin. . . .

Pulau Ubin is a lovely place to walk, birdwatch, camp, trek, bike, fish, fly kites or dine. Try to allow a full day here with lots of sunblock and water. Quarries on the island were once the source for much of Singapore's granite for the causeway and early skyscrapers. Its name supposedly derives from the Javanese word for "squared stone". The *kampong* seems unchanged since the 1950s. There's an interesting bungalow (although a little hard to find) on the eastern end of the jungle trails, best reached by bicycle (available for hire).

### Pulau Ubin
http://www.nparks.gov.sg/nparks_cms
To get to Pulau Ubin, take SBS Transit bus 2 or 29 to Changi Point. Walk across to Changi Jetty where bumboats leave frequently for Pulau Ubin. The journey takes about 10 minutes. Operating from 6am to 10pm daily, the boat will only leave the jetty when it is full with 12 passengers. The fare for a single trip is $2.00 and $4.00, if you are bringing a bike over. Free guided tours are conducted every fourth Saturday of the month.

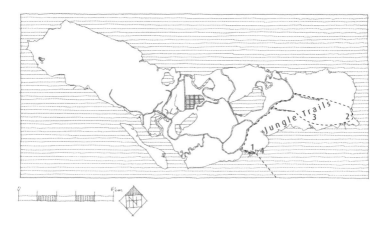

## Key: Pulau Ubin

1. Kampong Pulau Ubin
2. Bungalow
3. Kampong Surau Mosque
4. Pulau Ubin Coast Guard Police post

# Architectural Styles

This chapter explains some of the architectural styles mentioned in the book. It discusses the distinct shophouse and bungalow styles common to Singapore and outlines some popular architectural styles, such as Neoclassicism and Gothic. There are also notes on Chinese and Indian temples as well as Malay houses and mosques.

# Shophouses

## The Shophouse, 1840–1960

This definitive Singaporean building, widely constructed between 1840 and 1960, is typically a business premises with living quarters on the upper floors. Traditionally, the width of the shophouse depended on the length of felled timber available (typically 5 m). The five-foot-way (1.5 m), formed by the overhanging upper storeys, is credited as Raffles' innovation, providing shade from daytime heat and the constant threat of rain, enabling trade to be carried out in relative comfort. Many of these five-foot-ways are paved in slippery tiles.

Five-foot-way

There are five different shophouse styles. Roughly chronologically, they are: Early, First Transitional, Late, Second Transitional and Art Deco. Chinatown, Little India and Kampong Gelam all have their own variations, with Kampong Gelam's being the most flamboyant. The adoption of classical elements on façades remained a constant, but they were often colourfully painted. The Chinese, Peranakans and Malays loved colour, believing it brought good luck. Black and white, favourite colours of the expatriate British for their bungalows, was anathema to the Chinese, since it was associated with mourning.

## Early Style Shophouse

Example: Tanjong Pagar Rd

The Early Style Shophouse was the first type of shophouse to be built in Singapore and was never higher than two-storeys, with little or no decoration. It also usually did not have very high ceiling. In common with all subsequent shophouse styles, the Early Style had a five-foot-way, which ran along the front of the original business premises, above which the residential accommodation was located. Early Style shophouses usually had no more than two windows, which were often shuttered with jalousies, overlooking the street.

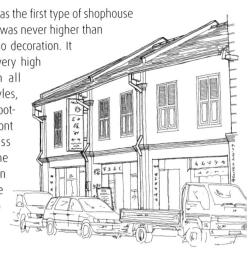

Tanjong Pagar Rd

61 Serangoon Rd

## First Transitional Style Shophouse, Early 1900s
Example: 61 Serangoon Rd

This style looks generally less solid and squat than the Early Style shophouse, which it follows, due to significantly taller storey heights and because openings are roughly equal to wall space. There are usually only two windows on the upper floor (but often there's a third storey). There's more ornamentation but it's still relatively restrained, the columns, usually modified Corinthian or Composite, are more decorative while vents above or between windows can be quite elaborate.

## Late Style Shophouse
Example: Kandahar St

The Late Style Shophouse was the most extravagantly decorated of all the shophouse styles. It had its heyday in the decades around the turn of the

Kandahar St

twentieth century and is perhaps the most easily recognized (and certainly the most commonly illustrated on posters and in guidebooks) shophouse style. This style is characterised by a bizarre mix of misunderstood neoclassical motifs, but its exhuberance makes up for any failings it might have on that score. Different parts of the city, such as Chinatown and Kampong Gelam had their own individual twists on the classic three-storey, three bay design, but it was in Little India that this shophouse style was the most imaginative and expressive, particularly along Jalan Besar and Petain Rds. They were, and still are, painted bright colours, and it is lovely to see so many of them being restored and colourfully repainted after so many decades of decay.

## Second Transitional Style Shophouse, Late 1930s

Example: 45 Niven Rd

45 Niven Rd

Seen as an aesthetic reaction to the ornate Late Style shophouse, this relatively short-lived style could have simply been a result of the depressed economic situation at the time. It retains the three window openings of the Late Style but looks more austere because a lot, though not all, of the ornamentation is lost. A combination of Late Style shophouse motifs, such as ornately carved transoms and colourful ceramic tiles, were still employed, along with art deco elements like cross-braced glass window panels and simple geometric balustrade designs.

## Art Deco Style Shophouse, 1930–1960

Example: Bukit Pasoh Rd

30 Bukit Pasoh Rd

The latest of the shophouse styles, this is typified by clean lines and the streamlining of classical motifs (such as column orders, arches, keystones and pediments) into geometric designs. For instance, the column capital could be reduced to a simple circle motif. Decorative wall tiles are rarely used. It's a logical progression from the Second Transitional Style where proportion became more important than detail, and architects began to design groups of buildings rather than individual structures, paying particular attention to the corner houses. It became the fashion to install plaques with the building's date.

Pintu pagar: a small saloon-type half-door.

Swag & garland: a decorative carved or moulded feature which looks like a garland of leaves suspended between 2 pieces of draped cloth.

# Chinese Temples

The form of the traditional Chinese temple is usually based on that of a large house or palace, consisting of a group of pavilions arranged around open courtyards. Even the most recent temple constructions will follow methods that have changed little over the centuries. They are also built in strict accordance with the precepts of feng shui in an attempt to achieve a balance between the temple's Yin and Yang elements. Location also plays an important part in the decision to construct a Chinese temple, i.e. situating it close to water or halfway up a hill will lend it favourable feng shui.

Usually dedicated to one specific deity, Chinese temples can also be dedicated to more than one god, and some are even syncretic, which means that any number of different Chinese faiths (Buddhist, Taoist, Animist, etc.) are welcome to worship there.

The temple's layout (often on axial lines), with its sequence of courtyards and worship halls, reflects the Chinese etiquette of *li*, (the manner of humbling oneself in deference to others). They are rich in gilt-covered decorative carvings, mouldings and murals (usually imported from mainland China), often with the dragon as a prominent decorative feature.

Hu lu: A half-gable, half-hip roof; a feature of Chinese temple architecture.

Thian Hock Keng Temple, Telok Ayer St

Architectural Styles

# Gothic Style

This architectural style was common in Europe, particularly northern Europe, in the 12th to 16th centuries. Its main characteristic was the pointed arch. The Gothic style experienced a revival from the middle of the 18th century onwards, partly as a reaction to centuries of neoclassicism — a style that was more restrained, even dull — but mainly thanks to the huge popularity of Gothic novels. A battle raged between the Gothic and Classical styles throughout the 19th century in Europe and even in Singapore. The Gothic never really caught on here, except for a few religious and educational buildings.

The Composite order was popular in Singapore as it allowed for more flexibility of artistic expression than the Corinthian, which it resembled. It also allowed for the incorporation of local flowers and even animals.

Detail, Chijmes

# Bungalows

Strictly speaking, a bungalow is a single-storeyed house but, in Singapore, it means any freestanding residence. Derived from the word *bangala*, the traditional Bengali mud-walled house, bungalows were built by the British in Singapore and Malaya (Malaysia) from the 1830s.

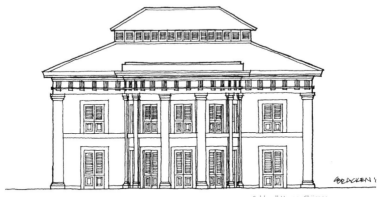

Caldwell House, Chijmes

### The Early Style Bungalow

The Early Style bungalow, which had its heyday in the 1860s, was often single-storeyed, raised off the ground by brick piers or timber posts for air circulation. Generally symmetrical, with a front portico (*anjung*), high ceilings and a verandah (*serambi gantung*), the kitchen (*kapor*) and servants' quarters were at the rear and were separated from the main house with their own external staircases.

### The Victorian Bungalow

The Victorian bungalow, popular in the 1870s, was built solidly, using load-bearing brick walls. It was also considerably larger and more decorative than other styles, with turrets, ornamental columns, ironwork and decorative plasterwork consisting of pendants, swags, garlands and plaques.

### The Black-and-White Colonial Bungalow

The black-and-white colonial bungalow, named after the exposed half timbers which hinted at Tudor architecture, was built from 1900 until just before World War II. It eschewed all ornamentation and reverted to the use of an encircling verandah, perhaps the best known and certainly the most attractive of the colonial house styles.

759 Mountbatten Rd

### The Art Deco Bungalow

The Art Deco bungalow, built during the 1920 and '30s, had a different layout from the earlier styles, the emphasis being on family living, with the kitchen and servants' quarters being brought into the main house. Constructed of concrete, it was strongly

23 Nassim Rd

horizontal in design. Classical motifs were used, as were flat roofs and curved corners. The Early Modern Style bungalow was a 1950s version of art deco. It was also strongly horizontal in design, with flat roofs and curved corners but with even less decoration. The two styles are so similar that they are virtually indistinguishable.

### The Postmodern Bungalow

The Postmodern bungalow, at best, is a style that playfully and ironically takes classical elements and reinterprets them using modern materials, often surprisingly, as many of the components were originally designed in an industrial context. Bright colours are also frequently used. Sadly, there aren't that many good examples of this style in Singapore, although KNTA Architects have produced some attractive examples on Cluny Park Rd, just north of the Botanic Gardens, and farther north at Corfe Place.

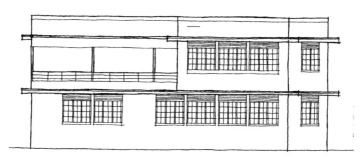

745 Mountbatten Rd

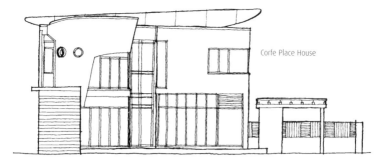

Corfe Place House

# Neoclassicism

Classical architecture flowered in ancient Greece and Rome in the centuries before and after the birth of Christ. As a style, it was elegant and harmonious, but it disappeared with the fall of the Roman Empire. It was revived in the 17th century, first in Italy and then throughout the rest of Europe, largely thanks to Andrea Palladio, an Italian architect who studied the ruins of ancient Rome and adapted their styles to suit his era.

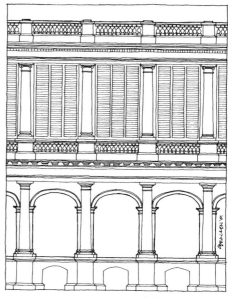

The Istana

With the spread of the European empires, this style became global. In Singapore, a "Coarsened Classicism" gradually emerged, particularly in its shophouses. It was named as such because the application of the classical elements tended to be haphazard, sometimes even crude, and used mainly for their decorative effect with little or no understanding of the rules. The Istana is a good example of a building in the neoclassical style that follows the rules well.

Neoclassicism was popular in Singapore for government buildings, as it was in most of the British colonies right up until the outbreak of World War II. Yet the Gothic style reigned supreme in the United Kingdom itself during the same period. It was often the younger sons of well-to-do families who went to the colonies to seek their fortunes. They were usually classically educated and favoured the neoclassical style. The Gothic style was the preferred architectural style of the self-made industrialists from the North of England who began to have more of a say in the running of the United Kingdom as the 19th century wore on, influencing the style of government buildings, including the Houses of Parliament at Westminster.

Doric

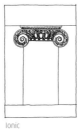

Ionic

The Istana follows the precedent set by the Colosseum in Rome, where the first floor uses the Doric order, and the second, the Ionic.

# Indian Temples

Singapore has a number of important Hindu temples dotted throughout the city and suburbs. Elaborately sculpted, they stand out in all their technicolour glory. Always square-shaped in plan (Hindus regard the square as the perfect shape), a complex set of rules governs the site, design and building of every temple. These rules are based on numerology, astronomy, astrology and religious law, and are so complicated that it's customary for each temple to keep its own set of calculations, almost as if they were religious texts. Each temple is dedicated to a particular god. Temples are a constant hub of activity and a focal point for the Hindu community, who gather to celebrate many different rites and festivals. When visiting a Hindu temple, remember to dress conservatively and to remove your shoes before entering.

Chettiar Temple, Tank Rd

## Mosques

Mosques are dotted all over Singapore. Malays were the original inhabitants of the island, and their faith was primarily Islam. Mosques will usually have at least one minaret from which the *muezzin* will call the faithful to prayer, though nowadays the human voice is often replaced by broadcast recordings. Sometimes they also have a dome. Decoration can be colourful and elaborate, often consisting of intricate geometric patterning since portrayal of images is forbidden. Remember when entering a mosque to leave your shoes outside, and that you must be dressed appropriately — no shorts or singlets allowed — this is especially important for women.

Malabar Mosque

# Malay Houses

Malay House

Traditional rural Malay communities were centred around *kampongs* (villages). The *kampong*'s shape and extent originally depended on the hearing distance of the drum (later, the call of the *muezzin*) at the mosque which summoned people to prayer. *Kampongs* developed along streams and rivers which were liable to swell after tropical rainfalls, so, unlike in India or China, the traditional Malay house was raised off the ground on wooden stilts about 1.5 m–2.4 m (5–8 feet) above the ground.

Three elements distinguished the Malay house: the stilts on which it stands; its open plan, usually consisting of the core house (*rumah ibu*), to which the kitchen (*rumah dapur*) was attached; and its pitched roof. The main room was used by the family for meals and to gather, and was converted at night into sleeping quarters. Roof styles differed from place to place, but were usually covered by ironwood (*belian*) shingles, allowing a continuous airflow through the house to keep the interior cool. Wooden pegs were preferred over iron nails.

There are very few Malay houses left in Singapore. Most of these are in Pulau Ubin, where they are in their natural setting. You can also visit the Geylang Serai Malay Village at 39 Geylang Serai to see some examples. The nearest MRT station to the village is Paya Lebar. The following bus numbers go there: 2 (from the East), 7 or 13 (from Orchard Rd) , 24 (from the airport) and 30 (from Jurong).

Anjung: Malay word for portico, which is a structure consisting of a roof supported by columns or piers, usually used as a porch.

# Glossary

| | |
|---|---|
| *anjung* | portico (Malay word). |
| **arcade** | a long arched gallery or verandah, often open at only one side, formed by a series of arches supported by columns or piers and quite decorative. |
| **arch** | curved structure over opening. |
| *attap* | thatch. |
| **baba** | Peranakan male. |
| **baluster** | short post supporting a handrail. |
| *belacan* | prawn paste. |
| *belian* | shingles/wooden roof tiles. |
| *bendahara* | Malay village leader. |
| **blood and bandage** | alternating bands of white plaster and red brickwork. |
| **breeze block** | perforated block used for ventilation, often ceramic and decorative. |
| *bukit selegie* | a type of Malay spear. |
| **bungalow** | large, detached villa (Singaporean usage). |
| **buttress** | projecting wall support. |
| **capital** | head of a column or pillar. |
| *chatri* | small onion-shaped dome, a feature of Hindu temple architecture. |
| *chulias* | Muslim merchants from South India. |
| **colonnade** | row of columns (similar to an arcade). |
| **cornice** | ornamental moulding, usually running near the top of a wall. |
| **cupola** | small dome. |
| **dentils** | small, square decorative blocks. |
| **fascia** | long, flat board, usually wood, covering the ends of rafters. |

| | |
|---|---|
| **feng shui** | arrangement of buildings or furniture to ensure good fortune for the inhabitant. |
| **fretwork** | timber cut in a decorative and often repeating pattern. |
| **gable** | triangular upper part of a wall at the end of a roof. |
| *gopuram* | colourful and elaborate decorative structure over Hindu temple entrances. |
| **godown** | warehouse. |
| *haji* | male Muslim who made the pilgrimage to Mecca. |
| *hajjah* | female Muslim who made the pilgrimage to Mecca. |
| **hip-roof** | a roof having sloping ends and sloping sides. |
| *hu lu* | a half-gable, half-hip roof and a feature of Chinese temple architecture. |
| *istana* | palace (Malay word). |
| **jack roof** | small roof separated from the main roof for ventilation purposes. |
| **jalousie** | shutter with fixed or moveable slats. |
| *kampong* | Malay village (spelt kampung in Malay). |
| **keystone** | central stone in an arch. |
| *keramat* | Malay/Muslim shrine |
| *kongsi* | Chinese clan association (Chinese word). |
| *li* | correct behaviour, often an attitude of humbling oneself in deference to others (Chinese word). |
| **loggia** | open-sided arcade, often on an upper floor. |
| **motif** | design element which is repeated. |

| | |
|---|---|
| **Nanyang** | South Seas (Chinese word). |
| **nyonya** | Peranakan female. |
| ***orang laut*** | Malay fishermen (Malay word). |
| **parapet** | portion of wall above roof. |
| **pediment** | type of gable, often over a portico. |
| **Peranakan** | Chinese Malaysian traditional culture, a person from that culture. |
| **pilaster** | an upright rectangular pier, which looks like a pillar attached to a wall. It can be load-bearing but, on Singapore shophouses, it tends to be applied as a decoration. |
| ***pintu pagar*** | small half door (saloon type). |
| **plinth** | square slab at the base of a column or support for a decorative architectural element, e.g. vase, statue, obelisk. |
| **portico** | roof supported by columns, usually forming an entrance. |
| **quoin** | cornerstone. |
| ***rumah dapur*** | kitchen (Malay word). |
| ***serambi gantung*** | verandah (Malay word). |
| ***sinseh*** | Chinese traditional medical practitioner. |
| **swag and garland** | decorative carved or moulded feature which looks like a garland of leaves suspended between two pieces of draped cloth. |
| ***temenggong*** | Malay chief. |
| ***tong*** | Chinese secret society. |
| **transom** | horizontal bar across a window or at the top of a door. |
| **wat** | Thai temple. |

Glossary

# Listings

## CHINATOWN EAST

**Tea Chapter (Tea Museum and Shop)**
9a–11a Neil Rd. Tel: 6226 1175
Open from 11am to 11pm daily

**Public Gallery, URA Centre**
2nd floor, URA Centre. 45 Maxwell Rd. Tel: 6321 8321
http://www.ura.gov.sg
Open from 9am to 4:30 pm, Mon–Fri and 9am to 12:30 pm, Sat.
Admission: Free

**Chui Eng Free School**
131 Amoy St. Tel: 6532 7868
Open from 10am to 10 pm daily.
Admission: Free

**Fuk Tak Ch'i Temple Museum**
76 Telok Ayer St. Tel: 6532 7868
Open from 10 am to 10 pm daily.
Admission: Free

**Ying Fo Fui Kun**
98 Telok Ayer St
Open from 9am to 5pm, Mon-Sat
Admission: Free

# THE SINGAPORE RIVER

**UOB Plaza 1 Si Chuan Dou Hua Restaurant**
60th floor, UOB Plaza 1. 80 Raffles Place. Tel: 6535 6006

**Singapore Tyler Print Institute**
41 Robertson Quay. Tel: 6336 3663. http://www.stpi.com.sg
Open 9:30am to 8pm, Tue-Sat and 1pm to 5pm, Sun-Mon
Admission: Free

**Gallery Hotel**
76 Robertson Quay. Tel: 6849 8686. http://www.galleryhotel.com.sg
general@galleryhotel.com.sg

# FORT CANNING PARK

**Fort Canning Park & Centre • Cox Terrace • Fort Canning Park**
51 Canning Rise. Tel: 6332 1200 (for information on tours,
exhibitions and the hiring of grounds and facilities).
Offices open from 8:30am to 5 pm, Mon–Fri and 8:30am to 1 pm, Sat.
Admission: Free. Park is lit between 7pm and 7am daily.

**National Library**
91 Stamford Rd. http://www.nlb.gov.sg.
The library has been permanently closed from 1 April 2004

**Singapore History Museum (Riverside Point)**
30 Merchant Rd. Tel: 6332 5642. http://www.museum.org.sg/SHM
Open from 9am to 7pm, Tue–Sun and 1pm to 7pm, Mon
Late night opening till 9pm on Friday
Admission: Adult S$2, students (above 6 years) and senior citizens
(over 60) S$1. Free admission after 7pm on Friday
Free guided tours are available in English, Japanese, and Mandarin.
Check the museum website or call the museum for tour times.

Listings

### Asian Civilisations Museum, Armenian St

39 Armenian St. Tel: 6332 3015
http://www.museum.org.sg/ACM/acm.shtml
Open from 9am to 7pm, Tue–Sun and 1pm to 7pm, Mon
Late night opening till 9pm on Fri
Admission: Adult S$3, students (above 6 years) and senior citizens
(over 60) S$1.50. Free admission after 7pm on Friday
Free guided tours are available in English and Japanese.
Check the museum website or call the museum for tour times.

### The Substation

45 Armenian St. Tel: 6337 7535
http://www.substation.org

### Singapore Philatelic Museum

23B Coleman St. Tel: 6433 7347
http://www.spm.org.sg
Open from 9am to 7pm, Tue–Sun and 1pm to 7pm, Mon
Admission: Adult S$2, students (above 6 years) and
senior citizens (over 60) S$1.

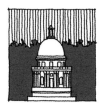

# THE PADANG

### Supreme Court Multimedia Gallery

1 St Andrew's Rd
Open from 8:30am to 5 pm, Mon–Fri and 8:30am to 1 pm, Sat
Admission: Free

### Parliament House

1 Parliament Place. Tel: 6332 6666
http://www.gov.sg/parliament
(Public entrance on Parliament Place)
Tours are available by appointment only. To enter the Strangers' Gallery when
Parliament is in session, Singaporeans require their I.C. and non-Singaporeans,
their passport, in exchange for admissions passes.
To enter the Strangers' Gallery when Parliament is in session, Singaporeans
need to bring along their I.C., and non-Singaporeans their passport.

### Asian Civilisations Museum, Empress Place

1 Empress Place. Tel: 6332 7798

http://www.museum.org.sg/ACM/acm.shtml
Open from 9am to 7pm, Tue–Sun and 1pm to 7pm, Mon
Late night opening till 9pm on Friday
Admission: Adult S$5, students (above 6 years) and senior citizens
(over 60) S$2.50. Free admission after 7pm on Friday
Free guided tours are available in English, Japanese and Mandarin.
Check the museum website or call the museum for tour times.

### Victoria Concert Hall & Theatre
9 and 11 Empress Place. Tel: 6333 0041. http://www.vch.org.sg or
Singapore Symphony Orchestra http://www. sso.org.sg
Tickets for most concerts and events in Singapore can be booked through:

**TICKET CHARGE**   Tel: 6296 2929. http://www.ticketcharge.com.sg
**SISTIC**   Tel: 6348 5555. http://www.sistic.com.sg

### The Esplanade: Theatres on the Bay
1 Esplande Dr. Tel: 6828 8377. http://www.esplanade.com
Tickets can be purchased through SISTIC.  Guided Tours available at S$8 (adults)
and S$5 (child aged 12 and below).

# BRAS BASAH ROAD
### Equinox
70th floor, Swissôtel The Stamford
Tel: 64316156 (Reservations)

### Raffles Hotel
1 Beach Rd. Tel: 6337 1886
http://www.raffleshotel.com

### Singapore Art Museum
71 Bras Basah Rd. Tel: 6332 3222
http://www.museum.org.sg/SAM
Open from 9am to 7pm, Mon–Sun
Late night opening till 9pm on Friday
Admission: Adult S$3, students (above 6 years) and senior citizens
(over 60) S$1.50. Free admission after 6pm on Friday
Free guided tours are available in English, Japanese and Mandarin.
Check the museum website or call the museum for tour times.

Listings

**The Action Theatre**
42 Waterloo St. Tel: 6837 0842
http://www.action.org.sg
info@action.org.sg

**Young Musicians' Society**
54–58 Waterloo St. Tel: 6332 5813
http://www.yms.org.sg

**Sculpture Square Limited**
Contemporary 3-D Art Centre
155 Middle Rd. Tel: 6333 1055
http://www.sculpturesq.com.sg

# KAMPONG GELAM
**Taman Warisan Melayu**
Housing a Museum of Malay Culture and History, performance areas, souvenir shops and ancillary facilities, including a Malay restaurant. Under the auspices of the Malay Heritage Foundation and the National Heritage Board, with the Public Works Department (now called CPG Consultants) acting as consultants. It is scheduled to open in December 2004.

# ORCHARD ROAD
**Istana**
http://www.istana.gov.sg/openhouse.htnl
Opened on some public holidays from 8am to 6.30 pm.
Dates are published on the website or in the local newspapers
Admission: Free for Singaporeans and Singaporean Permanent Residents. Others, including foreign visitors, are required to pay an entrance fee of S$1 per person.

# BOTANIC GARDENS

**Singapore Botanic Gardens**

Visitor Service Desk. 1 Cluny Rd. Tel: 6471 7361. http://www.sbg.org.sg
Open daily from 5am to midnight. Admission to Gardens: Free
Admission to National Orchid Garden: Adults S$2,
students (under 12) and senior citizens (over 60) S$1

# FURTHER AFIELD

**Sun Yat Sen Nanyang Memorial Hall**

12 Tai Gin Rd (off Ah Hood Rd along Balestier Rd). Tel: 6256 7377
http://www.wanqingyuan.com.sg/english
Open from 10am to 5 pm Tues–Sun. Opens until 10pm on Sat.
Admission: Adult S$3, students and senior citizens S$2.
Nearest MRT: Toa Payoh. Then take SBS Transit bus Nºs: 21, 130, 131, 139,
145 or 186 to Balestier Rd. If you take bus Nºs 139 or 145, alight at the third
bus stop after the Toa Payoh Interchange. Alternatively, take Nºs 21 or 131
from Thomson Rd (opposite the Novena MRT station) and alight at Balestier
Rd (opposite the Moulmein Community Centre).

**Alkaff Mansion Restaurant**

10 Telok Blangah Green. Tel: 6415 4888

**Pulau Ubin**

http://www.nparks.gov.sg/nparks_cms
To get to Pulau Ubin, take SBS Transit bus 2 or 29 to Changi Point. Walk across
to Changi Jetty where bumboats leave frequently for Pulau Ubin. The journey
takes about 10 minutes. Operating from 6am to 10pm daily, the boat will
only leave the jetty when it is full with 12 passengers. The fare for a single
trip is $2.00 and $4.00, if you are bringing a bike over. Free guided tours are
conducted every fourth Saturday of the month.

Listings

# List of Illustrations

## Chinatown West

## Chinatown East

## Singapore River

## Fort Canning Park

List of Illustrations

# Botanic Gardens

# Further Afield

# Architectural Styles

# List of Maps

## Singapore

## Chinatown West

## Chinatown East

## Singapore River

## Fort Canning Park

## The Padang

# List of Icons

**Must See**
Pages: 18, 28, 40, 49, 52, 54, 62, 64, 66, 67, 72, 73, 74, 76, 82, 86, 104, 114, 128.

**National Monument**
Pages: 19, 20, 21, 22, 29, 30, 31, 32, 38, 41, 43, 51, 52, 54, 60, 61, 62, 64, 66, 73, 74, 76, 77, 78, 82, 83, 90, 94, 101, 103, 104, 110, 120.

**Good View**
Pages: 40, 72, 124, 127.

**See At Night**
Pages: 26, 40, 42, 43, 74, 78, 83, 105, 106.

**Drinking**
Pages: 26, 27, 31, 37, 38, 40, 42, 44, 67, 68, 72, 73, 74, 76, 78, 105, 106, 110, 111, 121.

**Eating**
18, 26, 27, 31, 37, 38, 40, 42, 44, 49, 67, 68, 72, 73, 74, 76, 78, 85, 90, 105, 106, 110, 111, 112, 114. 121, 127, 128.

**Shopping**
Pages: 18, 31, 37, 42, 44, 67, 68, 72, 73, 74, 78, 86, 90, 112, 121.

# Index